Business Initiatives

Graham White with Susan Drake

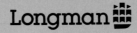

Longman Group UK Limited,
Longman House, Burnt Mill, Harlow,
Essex CM20 2JE, England
and Associated Companies throughout
the world.

First published 1989

Designed by Ken Brooks using MS
Word, Aldus PageMaker and Adobe
Illustrator Set in 10/12 Palatino on
Linotronic 300

Produced by Longman Group (FE) Ltd
Printed in Hong Kong

ISBN 0582 852692

Acknowledgements
The Publishers are grateful to the following for their permission to
reproduce photographs:
Art Directors Photo Library for page 23; Barnaby's Picture Library for
pages 3 bottom and 87d; The Body Shop for page 42; Camera Press
for page 42 bottom; J Allan Cash for pages 56, 87b, 87c, 87e, 119 and
125; Colorific for page 88 left; Greg Evans Picture Library for page 88
middle left; Robert Harding Picture Library for page 87a; Image Bank
for page 88 right; Dr. Jean-Pierre Lehmann for page 27; PIP Printing
for page 42; Picturepoint for page 3 top; Punch Publications Ltd for
pages 52 and 103; RCI Europe Ltd for page 85; Rex Features for page
79; Tony Stone Worldwide for pages 11, 47, 77, 88 middle right, 123 and
133; Tie Rack for page 42; Wimpy International for page 42 and
ZEFA Picture Library for page 70.

We are grateful to The New Yorker Magazine Inc. for their kind
permission to reproduce the following cartoons:
Page 22 (drawing by M Twohy © 1987); page 64 (drawing by M
Stevens © 1987); page 69 (drawing by R Mankoff © 1987); page 107
(drawing by C Barsotti © 1988) and page 128 (drawing by J
Stevenson © 1988).
The cartoon on page 28 has been reproduced by kind permission of
Tribune Media Services.

We are grateful to the following for permission to reproduce
copyright material:
BBC World Service for extracts from 'London Calling'; Epson (UK)
Ltd for and adapted extract from their advertisement in *The
Independent* 11. 10. 88; The Financial Times for adapted article
'Making the best of a precious resource' from *Financial Times* 7. 1. 85;
the Author, Godfrey Golzen, for an adapted extract from his article
'First Impressions Count' in *Drake Review* Vol 3, No 1, 1988;
Newspaper Publishing plc for adapted articles 'Managers urged to
work longer hours' by David Felton & 'Peak-time permits for cars to
enter London will be considered' by Terry Kirby in *The Independent*
19. 6. 87 & 3. 12. 87; Newspaper Publishing plc & the Author,
Jonathan Green-Armytage, a senior reporter with *Computer Weekly*
for an adapted extract from his article ' Digital Phone Revolution' in
The Independent 2. 11. 87; The Observer Ltd for an adapted extract
from the article 'The Holiday that's out of this World' by Martin
Bailey in *The Observer* 5. 88; Times Newspapers Ltd for an adapted
extract from the article 'It costs most to live in Lagos' by Patricia
Clough in *The Times* 1985.

Illustrated by Jerry Collins, Terry Grabbey, Frances Lloyd and
Edward McClachan.

Our special thanks to Athena International for allowing us to use the
premises for the cover photograph.

Cover photography by Con Putbrace.

To the student

Business Initiatives is designed to help you to learn the English you need for work. It presents English as an international language and the two cassettes contain American, British, German, French and Japanese people speaking English.

There are 16 main units, each based on a business theme. The units give you the opportunity to improve your speaking, listening, reading and writing. There is a *Language focus* section at the end of each of these units to help you with grammar.

In addition to the main units, Units 5, 10, 15 and 20 give you further skills practice in speaking, listening, reading and writing. Have a look at the Contents on the pages that follow for further details.

We hope you find *Business Initiatives* useful and that it helps you in your business career.

Graham White and Susan Drake

Contents

UNIT 1 *Excel worldwide*

In this unit you will:

- meet a visitor at the airport.
- talk about the area where you live.
- read about Excel's company structure.
- introduce a visitor to your colleagues.
- write a memo.

1.1 At the airport

 1 Nathalie Berthon, Excel Europe's Project Coordinator, is meeting Bob Peters at the airport in Lyon. Listen to their conversation and decide if these statements are **True** or **False**.

True	False	
✓		**1** This is Nathalie and Bob's first meeting.
		2 Bob suggests that they use first names.
		3 The plane was full so Bob didn't do any work.
		4 They are going directly to Excel's offices in the car.
		5 Nathalie takes one of Bob's suitcases.

1

2   Here's how to speak to people you meet for the first time.
In pairs, practise a conversation.

> Hello, I'm Bob Peters.
> Hello, my name's Bob Peters.
> Hi, I'm Bob Peters.
>
> You must be Nathalie Berthon.

> Yes, that's right.

> How do you do?
> Nice to meet you.
> Pleased to meet you.
> It's a pleasure to meet you.

> How do you do?
> Pleased to meet you too.
>
> Welcome to France.

> Thank you very much.
> I'm very pleased to be here.

> Did you have a good journey?
> How was the flight?

> Fine, thanks.
> No problems.
> It wasn't too bad, thank you.

> Can I help you with your baggage?
> Can I carry your case for you?

> Thank you.
> That's kind of you.

3   You are meeting a business contact for the first time. How would you answer these questions?

1 How do you do?
2 Do you speak English?
3 Did you have a good flight?
4 Can I carry your case for you?
5 Is this your first visit to Lyon?

Over to you   **4**   Now work in pairs. You are meeting your partner at the airport. The notes below and the conversation above will help you.

Student A

> Introduce yourself.
> Check your partner's name.

> Thank your partner.

> Tell your partner about the flight.

> Accept the offer of help.

Student B

> Confirm your partner is right.
> Welcome your partner to your country.

> Ask your partner about the flight.

> Offer help with the luggage/baggage.

1.2 On the way

1 Nathalie Berthon is driving Bob Peters to his hotel in the centre of Lyon.
Before you listen to their conversation, imagine you are Bob.
Which of these questions would you ask Nathalie?

1 How many people live here?
2 How much money do you earn a month?
3 Are you married?
4 What are the most important industries in Lyon?
5 What can you do in your free time?
6 Do you like living in Lyon?

● Can you think of any other questions to ask Nathalie?

 2 Now listen to the conversation between Bob and Nathalie and answer
these questions.

1 What's Lyon world-famous for?
2 What is Lyon's population?
3 What are the most important industries in Lyon?
4 Where does Nathalie come from?
5 What is the TGV?

Student B Ask your partner for information about Gothenburg.
Student A You are driving a visitor to the centre of Gothenburg in Sweden from the
airport. Tell your partner something about Gothenburg. The notes below
will help you.

Gothenburg
Attractions: Ship museum, botanical gardens, Liseberg Park (amusements
for children)
Distances: Stockholm 500 km / Frederikshavn (Denmark) 100 km by boat
Population: 500,000 (approx)
Economy: cars and trucks (Volvo), oil transport, port

Now change roles.

Student B This time you are driving a visitor to the centre of Milan in Italy from the
airport. Tell your partner something about Milan. The notes on page 133
will help you.
Student A Ask your partner for information about Milan.

3

1.3 All about Lyon

Here are some prepositions we use when we talk about places and travel.
Study them and complete the text about Lyon.

in south-west Germany	25 kilometres south **of** London	**on** the River Rhine
500 kilometres **from** New York	**near** the city centre	1 hour **by** train **from** Madrid
a population **of** about 500,000		

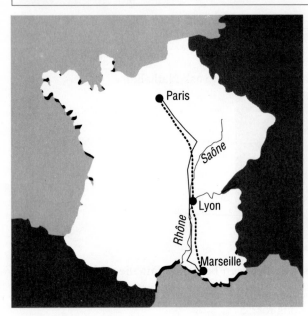

Lyon is .... central France .... the
Rivers Rhône and Saône, and has a population
.... about 1,200,000. It is situated 450
kilometres south-east .... Paris and is about
650 kilometres .... Marseille. Paris is only
two hours away .... train. The motorway
goes through the city centre and
communications with the rest of France are very
good.

● Now write about a city in your country
in the same way.

1.4 Reading about Excel

1   It is important for new employees at Excel to understand the organization.
Look at the map of the world and fill in the missing details from the
information in the Fact Sheet.

2   Find another expression or word in the Fact Sheet that can be used instead
of the words *in italic* in these sentences.

1 We employ *more than* 7,000 men and women worldwide.
2 The Group is in a strong position to *open* new markets.
3 Excel is now one of the *most important* manufacturers of electronics
  in France.
4 It has considerable potential for *increasing in size* in the future.

3   Find these adjectives in the Fact Sheet and add the nouns they describe.

1 original ....   4 wide ....
2 considerable ....   5 strong ....
3 main ....   6 interactive ....

● Now use these phrases in your own sentences.

EXCEL EUROPE FACT SHEET

Excel is now one of the leading manufacturers of electronics in France and a world leader in this area of technology. We have companies in Europe and North America, and we employ over 27,000 men and women worldwide.

If you look at this list of Excel's activities, you can see the role of your company in the organization:

The headquarters of Excel Europe are in Lyon where the original production plant still manufactures a wide range of electronics and communication products.

Macdonald Harris is in Livingstone, Scotland. Its main business is the manufacture of semiconductors and microchips, but it also makes satellite communication equipment.

Excel Germany, based in Frankfurt, produces telephone equipment, answering machines, and interactive communication systems.

Digital Communications (DC) is the youngest company in the group. It is a software engineering company based in Newbury, England. It has considerable potential for growth in the future.

In addition to these manufacturing companies, there are also sales and distribution companies in Spain, Sweden, Italy and Greece.

Excel Europe is part of the Excel Corporation, which has its head office in Boston, Massachusetts in the USA. The company has the largest share of the US semiconductor market.

With a worldwide sales operation and manufacturing companies in Europe and America, the Group is in a strong position to exploit new markets and develop new products.

David Latour
President

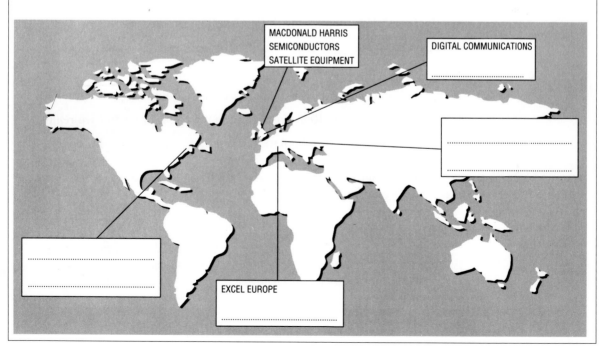

MACDONALD HARRIS
SEMICONDUCTORS
SATELLITE EQUIPMENT

DIGITAL COMMUNICATIONS

EXCEL EUROPE

1.5 Introductions

 1 Nathalie Berthon calls a meeting of her staff to introduce Bob Peters to
them. Listen to her and then answer these questions.

    1 What is Bob Peters' job title?
    2 Why is Bob Peters in France?
    3 How long is his visit?

 2 Now listen again and complete the dialogue.

Nathalie: OK, I think .... now. On behalf of everyone here, I'd

.... Bob Peters to Excel Europe. As ....,

Bob is the Product Manager with Excel in Boston. He's

.... to study our production methods and I'm

sure....................................... . Bob?

Bob: Well, thank you Nathalie. I'm .... to working with you all. We

hope to produce the XL10 in Boston in the next year or so and we really

need your know-how. I'm here to find out .... I'll be ...

Over to you **3** Welcome another visitor to Excel and introduce him or her to the office
staff. Here's an example.

> *Ladies and gentlemen, on behalf of everyone here, I'd like to welcome Klaus
> Jensen. Klaus is a software engineer working in the Sales Department of Excel
> Germany. He's staying with us for two weeks to train some of our computer
> operators. I'm sure we all wish him well.*

Name	Company	Job Title	Stay	Reason for visit
Klaus Jensen	Excel Germany	Software Engineer (Sales)	2 weeks	to train computer operators
Jane Crawford	Macdonald Harris	Management Trainee	1 year	to learn about the company
Miguel García	Excel Spain	Manager	1 day	to give a presentation of the CB4 system
Harold Goodman	Excel USA	Chief Executive	3 days	to attend a strategic planning meeting

1.6 Memo writing

1 Read this internal memo from Nathalie Berthon.

Internal memorandum

To: All production staff
From: Nathalie Berthon
Subject: Bob Peters' visit

This is to inform you that Bob Peters, Product Manager at Excel in Boston, is here for a six-week training visit.

Details of his schedule are attached. Please give him every assistance possible.

Thank you.

---

2 Write a memo informing staff of the visit of another employee from one of Excel's companies. Choose one of the people from the list above as your visitor.

1.7   On the spot

Here are some situations at the airport. Discuss with a partner what to say.

1 A stranger says 'Excuse me, do you know where I can change some money?'
2 At passport control, the officer says, 'What is the reason for your visit?'
3 You want to take a train to the centre of town. Ask at the Information Desk.

Here are some more situations, this time in a hotel. What do you say?

4 At Reception, the clerk wants to check your name. Spell out your name.
5 Ask about the arrangements for breakfast.
6 Ask if it is possible to use the hotel's fax. Ask for the fax number.
7 You want to hire a car for the weekend. Ask for details of cost and insurance.

Language focus – the Present Simple

1   We use the Present Simple to talk about facts and routines, e.g. *I **work** in the Sales Department. I **travel** abroad a lot.* It is also often used to talk about timetables and programmes in the future, e.g. *The train **leaves** at six.*

Don't forget that we add **s** to the third person form *(he/she/it)* of verbs in the affirmative, e.g. *He **trains** computer operators.*

If the verb ends in **-ch, -sh, -ss, -x** or **-o**, we add **es**, e.g. *She **goes** to Frankfurt every month.*

If the verb ends in a consonant **+y**, then the third person form ends in **ies,** e.g. *He **tries** too hard and **worries** too much.*

2   Fill the gaps in this paragraph about Nathalie Berthon. Use the verbs in the box in the Present Simple.

> work   be   speak   have   meet   understand   go   try

Nathalie Berthon .... Project Coordinator at Excel's Head Office in Lyon. She

.... with a team of six people. Excel .... offices and factories all over

the world and Nathalie regularly .... colleagues from other Excel companies.

She .... French, English, Italian, a little Spanish and .... a few words

of Swedish. She .... to attend an English course every week, but it

.... often difficult because there .... so much work to do. Once a year

she .... skiing.

● Describe your own job in the same way in about 50 words.

3   To ask questions and make negative statements using the Present Simple, we use the **do** form, e.g. ***Do** you **speak** French? No, I **don't**. **Does** she **work** for Excel? No, she **doesn't**. **Does** the exhibition **open** at nine or ten? Nine.*

Now ask your partner if he or she:

1 speaks Italian.
2 works for a multinational company.
3 travels to work by car.
4 uses a word processor.
5 goes skiing in the winter.

UNIT 2 *Nobody does it better!*

In this unit you will:

- compare different products and choose the best.
- read about time management.
- discuss priorities.
- exchange information over the phone.

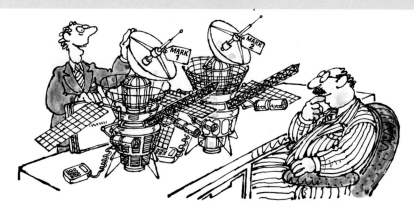

'But of course the Mark 2 is a little more expensive.'

2.1 Looking at the product

  1 Nathalie Berthon is showing Excel's latest product, the CB4, to Bruno Toti, a customer from Italy. Listen to their conversation. What do you think the CB4 is?

Use these phrases:
It could be ...   *It must be ...*
It might be ...   *It's probably a ...*
It can't be ...

  2 Listen again to the conversation and tick the correct box.

	CB3	CB4
bigger		✔
clearer		
heavier		
cheaper		
better sound quality		
more complicated		

3 Fill in the gaps in this passage.

The CB4 is a new *v*................ *p*................ *s*................made by Excel. It looks more *com*................ than the CB3 but in fact it is *e*................ to operate. Also, the *instr*................ *man*................ is more *u*................-*f*................

The *res*................ costs were high so the system is a little more *e*................ than the CB3. The picture and sound *qu*................ are excellent.

4 Can you say these words correctly? Underline the **stressed** syllable.

1 advanced	**5** expensive	**9** standard
2 system	**6** manual	**10** research
3 operation	**7** complicated	**11** simpler
4 improvement	**8** model	**12** quality

2.2 Which one?

1 Bruno Toti is looking for a videophone system for his company. He wants to link up his different offices and factory sites in Italy. Bruno looks at two other systems. Here are his notes.

	EXCEL CB4	IEC IE10	SVENSSON ALPHA XT
Design	8	8	7
Operation	7	5	6
Value for money	5	6	4
Picture quality	7	7	8
Sound quality	8	9	6
Manual	8	6	9

10 = Excellent   0 = Unacceptable

Check the grammar of making comparisons in the *Language focus* section on page 14. Then write sentences comparing the three models, e.g. *The IEC 10 is more difficult to operate than both the Svensson Alpha XT and the Excel CB4.*

Over to you **2** Here is part of Bruno's final report.

> Recommendation
> All the factors listed in the chart above are important, but, in deciding upon a new system, we must think carefully about the quality of both the sound and the picture. Also, we have to be very careful to keep the cost to a minimum. I must therefore recommend the .... as the best choice and hope that all the members of the Budget Committee will ...

In small groups, compare the systems and decide which one to buy.
You must give your reasons.

Here are some phrases to help you:

I think that ...   *I agree with you.*
In my opinion, the CB4 ...   *I don't agree about that.*

2.3 Managing your time

1 You are going to read an article about how to manage your time well.
Before you read it, think about a manager's job. Which of these jobs should
a manager normally do?

- answer the telephone
- sign letters
- write reports
- type his/her own letters
- make plans for the future
- deal with problems of his/her staff
- make tea or coffee
- answer routine letters

2 Now read the article. Answer the questions in it and underline **three** points
which will help you to improve your work.

MANAGING YOUR TIME

Do you waste time or use it efficiently?

The first rule of successful time management is to accept that there will never be enough time. So start with this thought: *Work smarter, not harder!*

To help you use your time more efficiently, first think about these questions:

1 Do you have an untidy desk?   YES/NO

2 Do you make and receive social calls at work?   YES/NO

3 Do you allow frequent interruptions to your work?   YES/NO

4 Are you always working to a deadline?   YES/NO

5 Do you *prioritize* ? Do you decide which jobs are
most important and do them first?   YES/NO

6 What percentage of your day do you spend on:
  ● coffee breaks?   ....%
  ● lunch hours?   ....%
  ● chatting to colleagues?   ....%

Keep a daily record of how your time is actually spent, whether it is 'work' or not. You can then discover the major timewasters.

  ● PLANNING is the key to effective time management.
  ● MAKE A PLAN for every month, every week, and every day.
  ● MAKE YOUR WEEKLY PLAN on Friday to avoid a cold start on Monday.
  ● TAKE 5 OR 10 MINUTES every morning to make your daily plan.
  ● PLAN 'FREE PERIODS' in which phone calls can be returned or people can come and see you.
  ● PLAN your coffee and lunch breaks to give a change of pace in the day. Long hours at your desk are not always productive.
  ● FINALLY, the good manager delegates as much routine work as possible.

3   Write the correct form of the words in capitals in the sentences.

1 What .... of your day do you spend on coffee breaks? PER CENT

2 Keep a .... record of how your time is actually spent. DAY

3 Planning is the key to .... time management. EFFECT

4 Do you waste time or use it ....? EFFICIENT

5 Long hours at your desk are not always .... PRODUCT

2.4 Priorities

To make a good decision in business you need two things:
- information.
- clear priorities.

You often have to decide which of two (or more) possible actions is more important or urgent and which is less important and can wait.

Imagine you work in the Sales Department and have an assistant and secretary working for you. You arrive at your desk one morning and find a pile of papers.

First, decide what action to take – the first one is done for you. Secondly, put them in an order of priority: *1* against the most urgent, *2* for the second, and so on. Work with a partner. You should delegate as much routine work as possible.

ITEM	ACTION	PRIORITY
1 telex from customer asking for quotation	*send telex*	....
2 note from Head of Department requesting urgent meeting	....	....
3 telephone message: customer has not received the goods due for delivery yesterday.	....	....
4 note from Chief Accountant: this month's sales figures for your department are two days late.	....	....
5 two application letters for post of trainee sales representative	....	....
6 telephone message: Mr Toti cannot come to appointment next Monday. Can he come this afternoon?	....	....
7 letter from Trade Fair organizer advertising Trade Fair next year in Singapore	....	....
8 four letters to branch offices for checking and signature	....	....

- Now explain why you selected this order of priority, e.g. *We decided to check and sign the four letters first to get them out of the way.*

2.5 On the spot – giving information over the phone

1 Giving information to another person over the phone can be difficult, especially if there are a lot of names and numbers. First, listen to this phone conversation and write down the message.

2 Listen again and make a note of the phrases for checking information and asking for help.

3 Work in pairs. Imagine you are speaking on the telephone.

Student A Take down the information Student B gives you and then give him/her your information.

Student B Give your partner the information on page 133 and then take down the information he/she gives you.

Student A Give this order over the phone to Student B.

> Order from Pan Arab Air Cargo Company for 2 Excel PKX audio communication systems (Catalogue No. 87960 - 84) Price $1,250 each including freight.

Language focus – Comparatives and Superlatives

1 *Short adjectives*
(one-syllable and two-syllable adjectives ending in **-er**, **-le**, **-ow**, **-y**)

Add **-er** for the comparative, e.g. *clearer*
Add **-est** for the superlative, e.g. the *clearest*

Spelling

If the adjective ends with a short vowel and a single consonant, double the consonant, e.g. *big* → *bigger*
            the biggest

-y changes to -i, e.g. *easy* → *easier*
            the easiest

2 *Long adjectives*
(all other adjectives with two or more syllables)

Comparative: put **more** or **less** before the adjective.

Superlative: put **the most** or **the least** before the adjective.

e.g. ***more*** *expensive*   *less* *user-friendly*
the most *expensive*   **the least** *user-friendly*

But note

good ➜   *better* ➜   *the best*
bad ➜   *worse* ➜   *the worst*

3   *As ... As*

We can also compare advantages and disadvantages of things in this way:

The CB4 is **as** *popular* **as** *the CB3.*
The CB4 is not **as** *heavy* **as** *the CB3.*
The CB4 is not **as** *cheap* **as** *the CB3.*
The CB3 is not **so** *expensive* **as** *the CB4.*
The CB4 is not **so** *well-known* **as** *the CB3.*

Note that the **So ... as ...** combination is only possible in negative sentences, e.g. you **cannot** say *The CB4 is* **so** *popular* **as** *the CB3.*

4   *Qualifiers*

We can show how big the difference is between the things we compare by using adverbs.

big differences

The CB4 is **much** *more expensive than the CB3.*
The CB3 is **a lot** *heavier than the CB4.*

small differences

The CB4 is **a little** *more expensive than the CB3.*
The CB3 is **a bit** *quieter than the CB4.*

5   Write six sentences comparing these two Italian hotels. Use these adjectives: *comfortable, expensive, near, large, noisy, friendly.*

Say whether the difference between the hotels is big or small.

★ ★ ★ ★	★ ★ ★
HOTEL ALESSIO	**HOTEL LIGURIA**
Lire 100,000 per night	Lire 75,000 per night
2 minutes from the sea	10 minutes from the sea
80 rooms, near a park	25 rooms, near the airport
Belongs to an international chain of hotels.	Owned and managed by one family.

15

In this unit you will:

- talk about plans and arrangements.
- welcome an overseas visitor.
- make, accept and refuse offers.
- read about the Pacific Basin.
- make contact over the phone.

3.1   On the way to Seoul

1 Bill Caxton of the Excel subsidiary, Macdonald Harris, is on a flight to Seoul. He meets an ex-colleague, Franco Toncini. Listen to their conversation and note down:

1 Bill's position in Macdonald Harris.
2 why he is flying to Seoul.
3 where he is flying on to later and why.
4 where he is staying in Seoul.
5 how long he is staying in Seoul.

2 Fill in the gaps in the passage about Franco, using the words in the box.

> Franco is an executive .... for a company based in Turin, Italy. He is ....
> an important customer in Seoul who is .... problems with one of his company's
> products.
>
> After that, he is .... on to Singapore where he is .... to find a company
> to .... parts for a new machine. He is .... to Turin after his stop in
> Singapore. Franco is .... at the Seoul Sheraton for three nights and he is
> .... to go out for a meal with his friend Bill tomorrow evening.

> having   working   planning   visiting   flying
> returning   hoping   staying   supply

Over to you 3 You are on a flight to the US when unexpectedly you meet an old friend. What do you say? Work with a partner. Tell him or her where you are going and why.

Look at the *Language focus* section on page 22 if you need help with the Present Continuous forms.

3.2 Welcome to Seoul

1 Bill Caxton is with Kim Lim of Sungpen, a large Korean trading company. The two men have never met before. Bill wants to buy components for a new range of Excel products. But before they get down to business, they have a general conversation and get to know each other a little.

What would you ask Bill Caxton in this situation? Write down some of the questions you would ask a business visitor.

2 Now listen to their conversation. How many of Kim Lim's questions did you guess correctly?

Over to you **3** You are welcoming a visitor from Taiwan to your company. Work with a partner. Use some of the phrases you noted down from the dialogue.

- Offer your partner hospitality (*food and drink*).
- Ask if it is your partner's first visit to your country.
- Ask your partner about his/her journey to your country.
- Ask how long and where s/he is staying.

3.3 A busy schedule

1 After their meeting Kim Lim asks about Bill Caxton's plans for the rest of the day. Listen to their conversation and note down the arrangements they make about:

1 giving Bill technical specifications.
2 lunch today.
3 dinner this evening.
4 a visit to the factory tomorrow.
5 Bill's journey to the airport tomorrow.
6 a taxi back to the hotel this afternoon.

2 Look at these sentences from the conversation. Fill in the missing prepositions.

1 I'm very impressed .... your product range.

2 I've got another appointment .... twelve .... the other side .... the city.

3 Are you free .... dinner this evening?

4 My flight leaves .... three pm.

5 I can arrange .... our courtesy car to take you out .... the airport .... one o'clock.

3 Here are some ways to make an offer. Complete the sentences from the conversation.

1 Would you like to ...?   3 Would you like me to ...?
2 Shall I ...?   4 Can I offer you ...?

18

4   Now work in pairs.

Student A   You are responsible for arranging the visit of a guest from Taiwan. Offer the following things and note down what the visitor, Student B, would like to do. Use the phrases above.

- a tour of the factory
- a sightseeing tour of the city
- a demonstration in the R&D department
- a meeting with the Overseas Sales Director
- lunch in a local restaurant
- use of the company courtesy car
- a view of a video promotion film

Student B   You are the visitor from Taiwan. Decide which of the things offered you want to accept. If you decide to refuse something, give a reason.

3.4   The Pacific Basin

1   On the plane, Bill Caxton picked up an in-flight magazine and read an article about the Pacific region. What do you know about the manufacturing industries in this region?

2   Now read the article and find out:

1   the names of two countries which have fast-growing economies.
2   the name of one country which offers a large market.
3   the name of the leading country in the area.
4   the number of countries in the Pacific Basin.
5   four types of natural resources in the area.
6   the reasons behind the growth in manufacturing in that area.

THE PACIFIC – AREA OF ECONOMIC GROWTH

The 34 countries round the Pacific Basin and the 23 island states in its 70 million square miles account for more than half the world's population and half its total wealth. The Pacific Basin has 21 per cent of the world's oil resources, 63 per cent of its cotton, 87 per cent of its natural rubber and 94 per cent of its natural silk. There are more than a thousand languages in the region and some of the richest religious and cultural traditions in the world.

In recent years, Taiwan has had the fastest-growing economy in the world. South Korea expects to be the fifteenth richest country in the world by the year 2000. And China is a vital and potentially vast new market. As these countries start to manufacture more complex products, they require more advanced technology.

The leader in this area has, of course, been Japan, which has exported not just its goods and services, but also its business expertise to the rest of the world. Following Japan's example, South Korea too is moving ahead at a speed that keeps costs, productivity and product quality one step ahead of the competition.

The reasons behind the growth of manufacturing in these Pacific nations are similar. They all have an educated and skilled labour force, willing to work long hours.

Strategically located on trade routes vital to both East and West, the Pacific Basin has enormous potential, as the West is beginning to realize.

3   Spot the error. One word in each of these sentences is wrong. Can you
replace it with the correct word? Here's an example.

There are 34 countries ~~under~~ the Pacific Basin.   ^round^

1   The Pacific Basin has 21 per cent of the world's oil researches.
2   It has some of the richest religious and cultural translations in the world.
3   China is a vital and potentially vain new market.
4   These countries require more advanced techniques.
5   Japan has exported its business expansion to the rest of the world.
6   South Korea keeps costs, productivity and product quantity one step
     ahead of the competition.
7   All these countries have an educated and skilled legal force.

4   Tick those **adjectives** which can be used to describe the **nouns** in the
vertical column. The first one is done for you.

	low	high	cheap	expensive	good	poor
1 costs	✔	✔				
2 productivity						
3 product quality						
4 potential						
5 products						
6 production						

5   This graph shows percentage increases in the GDP. *(Gross Domestic Product)*
of five countries over a period of five years. Read the text describing the
graph and label the lines of the graph with the names of the five countries.

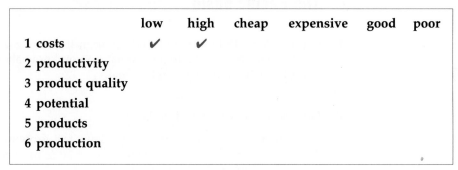

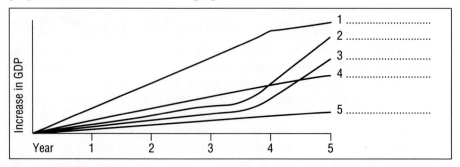

Of all the countries shown, Japan had the highest increase in GDP for four of the
five years. The United Kingdom's GDP grew but had the smallest increase overall.
The USA had steady, average growth.
   The newly industrialized Pacific Basin countries, South Korea and Taiwan, saw
low growth at the beginning of the period but in the final year, South Korea had
the biggest increase, with Taiwan only a little behind.

3.5 On the spot – getting through on the phone

You are on a business trip in the Far East. You make some telephone calls to arrange meetings. Fill in the gaps in these conversations.

1 You want to speak to Mr Chang.

Office: Chang Imports. Good morning.

You: ....

Office: Who's calling?

You: ....

Office: Putting you through.

2 You want to contact the Commercial Department.

Office: Department of Overseas Trade.

You: ....
Office: Sorry, the line is engaged. Will you hold?

You: ....

3 You want to speak to Mr Watanabe.

Office: Mr Watanabe's office.

You: ....
Office: I'm sorry, he's out at the moment. Can I take a message?

You: ....
Office: Thank you. I'll tell him.

4 You want to speak to Mary Wong. Check you have the correct office.

Office: Hello. Extension 344.

You: ....
Office: She's on another line now. Shall I transfer you?

You: ....

Language focus – the Present Continuous

"I'm not quite ready to order. My lawyers are still studying the menu."

1   We use the Present Continuous to describe what is happening now.

*What **are** you **doing** here?*
*I'm **flying** to Seoul, of course.*

2   We also use this verb form to talk about plans and arrangements we have made for the future.

*We're **having** dinner with Franco tomorrow.*
*Then we're **flying** on to Taiwan.*
*Are you **going** to the Hong Kong Trade Fair?*
*Are they **holding** the conference in France this year?*

3   Forward planning

Student B   Go to page 133.
Student A   Fill in your diary for the week ahead. Some appointments are already fixed. Then with Student B find a time when you can both meet to discuss next year's budget.

MON	1400 Marketing meeting
TUE	....
WED	10 30 R&D briefing
THU	....
FRI	....

UNIT 4 *East is East*

In this unit you will:

● ask and answer questions at a trade fair.
● write a telex.
● talk about work.
● make social contacts.

4.1 At the trade fair

1 Bill Caxton goes on from Korea to Singapore for a trade fair where he meets a Mr Cho. Listen to their conversation and answer these questions.

1 What is the name of the trade fair?
2 What is Bill interested in?
3 What is the history of the Singaporean company?
4 What overseas contacts does the Singaporean company have?

2 There are lots of useful business expressions in the conversation.
Listen again and fill in the gaps in these sentences.

1 Have you got any more ....?

2 .... to send you one if you'd like.

3 I'm simply trying to find out ....

4 ...., we manufactured transistors.

5 By the way, ...

6 .... if I do find myself in your area.

23

Over to you **3** Work with a partner. One of you is a visitor to Singatec who wants information from a software company with a stand at the fair. The other is the software company representative on the stand. Before you start, read the notes below and prepare what you are going to say.

Student A - the visitor to the stand

> Introduce yourself.
> Ask for a brochure.
> Ask for a translation in your own language.
> Find out something about the company.
> Say goodbye.

Student B - the representative on the stand

> Offer help.
> Hand over a brochure.
> Offer to send a translation as soon as possible.
> Ask for the visitor's address.
> Give the visitor general information about your software company.
> Say goodbye.

4.2 Two potential representatives

1 You visit a trade fair with a colleague. You both speak to as many people as possible, trying to find a suitable representative for your products. At the end of a busy day, you compare notes on two companies, Far East Trading and Asean Enterprises. Ask your partner to give you information about the other company.

Check the correct use of **much** and **many** in the *Language focus* section before you start.

Student B Go to page 134.

Student A Find out about Asean Enterprises and give Student B information on Far East Trading.

	FAR EAST TRADING	ASEAN ENTERPRISES
contact	Mr Chandra	
experience of agency work	20 years	
no. of employees	45	
no. of regular customers	600	
no. of sales staff	12	
marketing expertise	quite good	
contact with European companies	extensive	
impression	very professional	

2   Now that you have information about both companies, decide in pairs or small groups which company you are going to choose as your agent.

Here are some phrases to help you:

What do you think?
What's your view, ...?
I think we should ...
On the one hand, ... On the other hand, ...
Overall, I think that ...

4.3   Dealing with a telex

1   You are in the middle of a business trip in the Far East and are now in Hong Kong. You return to your hotel late on Wednesday evening and the receptionist gives you a telex from your Division Chief in Lyon.

ATTN: EXCEL REPRESENTATIVE
PROBLEM WITH DUBAI CONTRACT 1257/87. CANCEL ALL FURTHER VISITS IN HONG KONG AND
RETURN SOONEST.
CHECK FLIGHT AVAILABILITY AND ADVISE ASAP.
BRGDS CORBET
EXCEL LYON

---

1   Why must you change your plans?
2   What must you do now?

2 We use a lot of different abbreviations in telexes.
Match the phrases and abbreviations.

1	SOONEST	**A**	thanks
2	REYRTLX	**B**	as soon as possible
3	ASAP	**C**	as soon as possible
4	TKS	**D**	telephone conversation
5	CFM	**E**	for the attention of
6	BRGDS	**F**	confirm
7	TELECON	**G**	with reference to your telex
8	ATTN	**H**	best regards

3 You check the airline timetables and find that the first available flight is
tomorrow afternoon. Write the telex to Mr Corbet, giving him the
information he wants.

LH	**381**	**Dep. 1600**	**HONG KONG**	**Arr.**	**0555**	**FRANKFURT**
AF	**182**	**Dep. 0830**	**FRANKFURT**	**Arr.**	**0950**	**LYON**

4.4 How hard do you work?

1 Before you read the article, look at the title and discuss these questions with
a partner.

- How many hours do you work in a week?
- How many hours does the average office worker in your country work
  in a week?
- How many hours does the average factory worker in your country work
  in a week?
- How many days paid holiday do you have in a year?
- How much overtime do you work?

2   Now read the article and answer the questions which follow.

MANAGERS ADVISED TO WORK LONGER HOURS
by David Felton, Labour Editor

IF EUROPEAN INDUSTRY wants to be as efficient as the Japanese, then managers should work longer hours, go to the office on Saturday mornings and take only half their annual holiday. This advice was given to delegates attending the 13th annual congress of the European Association of Personnel Management in London this week by Professor Jean-Pierre Lehmann of the National Institute for Labour Studies. According to Dr Lehmann, this will help to stop Europe's declining level of productivity. More than that, it will make Europe wealthier and happier.

Jean-Pierre Lehmann

In his new working week for management at all levels, Dr Lehmann thinks that the managers should set an example and be at their work place from 8am to 6pm, with at least half a day on Saturday. Annual holidays should be similar to the American norm of two weeks. On the need for managers to spend time with their families, Dr Lehmann said, 'One can still spend a very good Saturday afternoon and Sunday with the family.'

Dr Lehmann accepts that many smaller, more dynamic companies are already working in this way and says that it is the bigger corporations that he is criticizing.

1   Who is Dr Lehmann?
2   What are his views on the working week?
3   What would be the results of the *new working week for management?*
4   Which companies are more likely to agree with Dr Lehmann, large companies or small companies?
5   Do *you* agree with Dr Lehmann?

3   Find words in the first paragraph which mean:

1   yearly.................   4   conference ....

2   falling   5   work ....

3   richer ....

4   Complete these phrases with a verb. They all appear in the article.

1   to .... time   4   to .... a congress

2   to .... an example 5   to .... a country wealthy

3   to .... a holiday

27

5 What are the important qualities of a manager? In groups, look at this list and decide which are important for a typical management job. Add ideas of your own.

QUALITIES	very important	important	not necessary
dynamic			
young			
well qualified			
experienced			
well liked			
self-motivated			
a natural leader			
a good communicator			
adventurous			
intelligent			
....			
....			

4.5 On the spot

1 One evening at Singatec, Bill Caxton goes into the bar. Listen to the conversation he has there with someone he has not met before. Write down the questions which keep the conversation going.

2 You are in the hotel bar. Someone comes over to your table. Start a conversation. Try to find out the following information about your partner: *name, job, nationality, reason for coming to the fair and what they think of it.*

Here are some phrases to help you in this kind of situation.

How long have you been here?   *I work for ...*
Would you like a drink?   *Pleased to meet you.*
My name's ...   *What do you think of the fair?*

Language focus 1 – Much and Many

1 Look at these sentences.

*Do you have **a lot of** experience in this area?*
*No, not **much**.*

***How many** customers do you have?*
*I can't give you a precise figure but quite **a lot**.*

To use **much, many** and **a lot of**, you must first be clear about the difference between **countable** and **non-countable** nouns. Look at these two lists.

Countable	**Non-countable**
(many/a lot of)	*(much/a lot of)*
customers	experience
agents	business
countries	time
products	production

Add these words to the correct list.

money	brochures	advantages	advice	equipment
software	details	information	programs	profits

2 Put **much, many** or **a lot of** into these sentences.

1 How .... companies do you have on your mailing list?

2 We haven't got .... time.

3 There aren't .... factories in the north-west of the country.

4 .... people follow in-company English courses.

5 There isn't .... industry near the coast.

6 Mr Toti has .... visitors this morning

Language focus 2 – Tag questions

1   In conversation, we often add tag questions to the end of sentences. The speaker uses tag questions to ask for confirmation or to check that he or she is right about something.

Here are some examples.

1 It's rather hot in here, isn't it?
   Yes, it is.
2 You've never been to Korea, have you?
   No, I haven't.
3 Mr and Mrs Thompson are very late, aren't they?
   Yes, they are.
4 Maria speaks Japanese, doesn't she?
   Yes, she does.
5 You don't know how to use this machine, do you?
   I'm afraid I don't.

From these five examples work out the rule for making tag questions.

2   Fill in the blanks in these questions and answers.

1 It's time to finish the meeting, ... ?

   Yes, ...

2 They haven't seen the photographs yet, ... ?

   No, ...

3 Anna understands Russian, ... ?

   Yes, ...

4 Mr and Mrs Stern will be coming to the reception .... ?

   Yes, ...

5 You work for EDC, ... ?

   Yes, ...

Focus on listening and speaking

5.1 International Report

Listen to the radio interviews with executives working in different parts of the world and indicate with a number (1, 2, 3 or 4) which one is speaking. The number is given to you in the first two sets of choices.

Franz Weber	(.1.)	is American.	(...)	
Mitsuo Ito	(.2.)	is German.	(.1.)	
Rosalba Piretti	(.3.)	is Japanese.	(...)	
Barbra Ford	(.4.)	is Italian.	(...)	

He/She works as	an executive in	(...)	an advertising agency.	(...)
	a sales representative in	(...)	a computer firm.	(...)
	a credit officer in	(...)	a beer company.	(...)
	a copywriter in	(...)	a bank.	(...)

He/She is	married with two children.	(...)
	unmarried.	(...)
	married without children.	(...)
	married with a new baby.	(...)

He/She lives in	an apartment building with one bedroom	(...)	which is
	a house with a garden	(...)	
	a modern flat with two bedrooms	(...)	
	studio in an apartment block	(...)	

in Turin	(...)	and which is	a 15 minute train journey	(...)	from work.
outside Tokyo	(...)		75 minutes by bus and subway	(...)	
in Los Angeles	(...)		a 25 kilometer drive	(...)	
in a village near Munich	(...)		a 10 minute drive	(...)	

He/She likes	cooking.	(...)	He/She has	five weeks'	(...)	holiday a year
	tennis.	(...)		two weeks'	(...)	
	jazz music.	(...)		one week's	(...)	
	gardening.	(...)		four weeks'	(...)	

and usually spends some of this time	by the sea.	(...)
	camping in France.	(...)
	visiting his wife's parents.	(...)
	in Hawaii or South America.	(...)

Special benefits from the company include	two cases of beer a month.	(...)
	shares after two years.	(...)
	a 5% housing loan.	(...)
	a salary above the average.	(...)

5.2 Finding out information

1   Work in pairs and use these prompts to help you interview your partner.

   1 what/your job?   ....

   2 who/work for?   ....

   3 you/children?   ....

   4 you/house or apartment?   ....

   5 how far/your work?   ....

   6 how many weeks/holiday?   ....

   7 where/go/holidays?   ....

   8 what/spare time?   ....

   9 you/extra benefits in your job?   ....

   10 what/like most/in your job ?   ....

   11 what/like least/in your job ?   ....

   ● Can you think of any other questions to ask your partner?

2   In *International Report*, you heard about the extra benefits or perks that a company can give its personnel. Make a list of any benefits that you can think of. Discuss these with your partner.

3   In *International Report*, Barbra Ford gives 4th July as an example of a national holiday in the USA. Here is a list of the US holidays.

★ ★ ★ ★ ★ ★	1st January	New Year's Day
★ ★ ★ ★ ★	3rd Monday in January	Martin Luther King's birthday
★ ★ ★ ★ ★ ★	3rd Monday in February	George Washington's birthday
★ ★ ★ ★ ★	Last Monday in May	Memorial Day
★ ★ ★ ★ ★ ★	4th July	Independence Day
	1st Monday in September	Labour Day
	2nd Monday in October	Christopher Columbus Day
	11th November	Armistice Day or Veterans Day
	4th Thursday in November	Thanksgiving Day
	25th December	Christmas Day

What are the main public holidays in your country? How many do you have in total? What do you usually do on them?

5.3   Open dialogue

1   Barbra Ford is welcoming you on a visit to her corporation in the United States. Complete your part of the conversations using these sentences.

That would be very interesting.   *Yes, it is.*
I'm pleased to meet you, I'm ...   *Thank you.*
Sorry I can't, I have another appointment. *Yes, that's right.*
No, I'm afraid I don't.   *That's very kind of you.*

Dialogue 1

Barbra Ford: Good morning. My name's Barbra Ford.

You: ....

Barbra Ford: Welcome to Los Angeles. This is your first visit, isn't it?

You: ....

Barbra Ford: Well, would you like to come and see round the plant?

You: ....

Dialogue 2

Barbra Ford: Now, our arrangements for tomorrow: we have a meeting at 8.30 with the Sales Department. Do you know how to get there?

You: ....

Barbra Ford: You can see it here on the map. Turn right at the entrance and it's the first building on the left.

You: ....

Barbra Ford: And in the afternoon, would you like to see our R & D department?

You: ....

Barbra Ford: What a pity! Perhaps next time. Well, I'll drive you back to your hotel.

You: ....

Barbra Ford: Don't mention it, it's a pleasure! You're staying at the Holiday Inn, aren't you?

You: ....

2   With a partner, practise

  1 welcoming him/her to your company.
  2 making arrangements.

5.4   Financial news

Listen to six news items.

Item 1   Complete the sentences below, choosing from these items.

Year - This year/Last year
Period - January to June/July to December
Results - Profit/Loss
Amount - £10.3 million/£12.5 million

During the period .... to .... of .... year Sun Data

results showed a .... of ....

This compares with a .... of .... for the period

.... to .... of .... year.

Item 2   Complete the information below with the figures you hear.

Value of digital exchange equipment ordered: £ ....

Cost of modernization programme: £ .... a year.

Value of Massey's shares: ....

Item 3   Answer the following questions.

Did the Dollar go up or down today?
How much did it change against the German Mark?
Were the US trade figures good or bad?
Did the Yen go up or down today?
Did the value of exports from Japan go up or down last month?

Item 4   Complete the information below with the figures you hear.

Old monthly interest rate ....%

New monthly interest rate ....%

New annual interest rate ....%

Item 5   Complete the information below with the figures you hear.

Number of overseas visitors to Britain in July ....

Number of North American visitors to Britain in July ....

Total spending by overseas visitors in July ....

Item 6   Underline the correct word or phrase to complete this report.

Metropolitan, the largest *theatre/cinema/supermarket* chain in the country has announced a *profit increase/profit decrease/loss* of *15%/50%/60%* for the past *3/ 6/12* months. The reason they give is the record rainfall this *year/spring/ summer*.

5.5   Programme choice

Here is part of a page from *London Calling* which gives you information on the programmes you can hear regularly on the BBC World Service.

1   Read the text and find out the titles of programmes on:

1 the arts	4 finance	7 pop music
2 science	5 books	8 sport
3 America	6 British politics	

2   Look at the text again. Make a list of four programmes which interest you. Compare and discuss your list with a partner.

SOME REGULAR PROGRAMMES
at a glance

Anything Goes – a variety of music and much more. Write to Bob Holness at World Service *Mons 0330 rep 080, 1331.*

Book Choice – short book reviews with three editions each week – *Suns 224 rep Tues 0540; Tues 1125 rep 2225; Weds 1740; Thurs 0140 rep 1125, 2225.*

Business Matters – a weekly survey of commercial and financial new *Fris 1230 rep 2130, Sats 0345.*

Classical Record Review – Edward Greenfield review new releases *Suns 1015 rep 1901, Weds 0815, Thurs 0430.*

Country Style – with David Allan *Weds 0145 rep Thurs 0815, Fris 0430.*

Development '88 – reflecting aid and development issues *Tues 1830 rep Weds 0730, 1330.*

Discovery – an in-depth look at scientific research *Tues 1001, rep Weds 0330, Thurs 1831.*

Europe's World – a magazine programme reflecting life in Europe and its links with other parts of the world F*ris 1215 rep 2115, Sats 1331.*

From Our Own Correspondent – BBC correspondents comment on the background to the news *Sats 2209 rep Suns 1315,0730, 1115.*

From the Weeklies – a review of the British weekly press *Fris 2315 rep Sats 0730.*

Good Books – recommendation of a book to read *Mons 0315 rep 0915, Weds 1945.*

Here's Humph! – all that jazz *Sats 0430 rep 1001, Thurs 1945.*

John Peel – selects tracks from newly released albums and single from the contemporary music scene around the world *Tues 0330 rep Thurs 0830, Fris 1330.*

Letter from America – by Alistair Cooke *Sats 1015 rep Suns 0545, 1645, 2315.*

Meridian – each week, three topical programmes about the world of the arts *Sats 0630 rep 1130, 2030; Tues 2030 rep Weds 0630, 1130; Thurs 2030 rep Fris 0630, 1130.*

Multitrack – all the latest news and music on the British pop scene *Mons, Weds, Fris 1830 rep Mons, Weds, Fris 2330; Tues, Thurs, Sats 1215.*

Nature Notebook – *Fris 1445 rep Sats 0145, 2225, Mons 1530.*

Network UK – looks behind the issues and events that affect the lives of people throughout the United kingdom. Three editions each week *Mons, Weds Fris 2101 rep Tues, Thurs, Sats 0215, 0745, 13300.*

New Ideas – a radio shop window for new products and inventions *Tues 0530 rep Weds 1730, Thurs 1115.*

Omnibus – each week a half-hour programme on practically any topic under the sun *Tues 1001 rep Weds 0330, 1001.*

The Pop Science Programme – *Tues 1001 rep Weds 0030, 1001.*

People and Politics – background to the British Political scene *Sats 1230 rep 1030, 2130.*

Personal View – of topical issues in British life *Fris 1945, Sats 0030, 0530,0945,*

The Pleasure's Yours – write to Gordon Clyde for your classical music requests *Suns 0815.*

Recording of the week – a personal choice from the new releases S*ats 0045 rep Mons 0545, Tues 1345, Weds 2145.*

Reflections – a daily consideration of the meeting point between religion and life *daily 0445 rep 0809,2240.*

Report on Religion – a weekly magazine of religious news and view *Tues 1945 rep Weds 0130, 0530, 1445.*

Science in Action – *Fris 1615 rep 2030, Suns 0915, Mons 0230.*

Seven Seas – weekly programme about ships and the sea *Thurs 2315 rep Fris 0745, 1015.*

Sports Round-up – *Mons-Sats following the 0930 Financial News, 1245; daily 1745, 2245, Suns only 1330.*

Sportsworld – the weekly sports magazine *Sat 1345, 1515, 1615.*

Talking From... – profiles from Northern Ireland, Scotland and Wales *Thurs 2101 rep Fris 0145, 1115.*

The Tony Myatt Request Show – *Sats 2315 rep Suns 1345.*

The Vintage Chart Show – past Top Ten hits with Jimmy Saville *Mons 1030 rep 2130, Fris 0330.*

Waveguide – how to hear us better *Suns 0750, Mons 0450, Tues 1115, Thurs 0130.*

Write On... – put your points to Paddy Feeny *Weds 2315, Thurs 1445, Fris 0730.*

3 Ask other members of your group some questions about listening to the radio and watching television.

Find out: • the number of hours of television they watch.
• the number of hours of radio they listen to.
• their favourite kinds of programme.

Are there programmes which your group all watch or listen to?

4 Follow-up – Personal listening exercise

You can practise and improve your understanding of spoken English by listening regularly to news programmes, for example, on the BBC World Service. (*Your teacher will help you to find the correct radio wavelength for your country.*) If you can, record the programme so that you play it several times in order to build up your understanding.

Here are some strategies for successful listening.

1 Choose a section of no more than five minutes of one programme.
2 Listen to the whole section first without stopping the tape.
3 Listen again and this time stop the tape and make notes of key words, people, places, figures, and so on.

5.6 What are you doing this weekend?

 1 Listen to these three people talking about their plans for the coming weekend, including Friday night. Make a note of their plans.

	Friday	Saturday	Sunday
Christina			
Martyn			
George			

Now write two or three sentences about each person's plans, using your notes.

2 Discuss these questions.

What do you usually do at the weekend?
What are you doing this coming weekend? The same as you always do or something different?
What do you enjoy most about weekends?

UNIT 6 *Reporting the facts*

In this unit you will:

- make an informal presentation.
- discuss information on graphs.
- write a short report.
- write a business letter.
- read about franchises.
- talk about the past.

6.1 The Fonex DB3

1 Klaus Jensen is a Software Engineer (Sales) for Excel Germany. He is in a meeting with Anna Persson, Purchasing Co-ordinator of the Svensaka Bank, at her Stockholm Office. The Svensaka Bank is interested in a new software package produced by Excel which will allow Svensaka customers to run their bank accounts from home.

Read the leaflet which Klaus Jensen sent to Anna Persson before their meeting. Note down:

1 the hardware you need at home to use the system.
2 other services available now.
3 new developments in the future.

FONEX DB3 THE ULTIMATE SOFTWARE PACKAGE

Fonex DB3 offers all the services big business expects from communications software packages – but now it's you, the domestic consumer, who will have all this information at your fingertips.

Fonex DB3 can be linked up with any domestic telephone. As soon as you are on line, you have access to a huge network of information and services through the Excel Superdatabase. All you need is your telephone, a TV set and the special Excel keypad to send and receive messages.

Fonex DB3 can help you to book a holiday, find out car prices, pay household bills ... the list is endless. And all from the comfort of your own home.

And that's not all - we'll soon be introducing a facsimile service and even videophones.

THE FUTURE. HERE TODAY WITH EXCEL.

---

2 Match the pairs to make correct sentences.

1 The Fonex DB3 is	**A** a new system from Excel.
2 You need the Excel keypad	**B** you have access to a lot of information.
3 Through the Superdatabase	**C** using the Fonex DB3 system.
4 You can use the system	**D** from communications software packages.
5 Business people expect a lot	**E** with any domestic telephone.
6 You can book a holiday	**F** to send and receive messages.

3 Put the correct word into these sentences. The first letter is given.

1 We plan to *i*........................ the equipment next week.

2 Domestic *c*.......................... will use the system.

3 We need fast *a*........................ to the information.

4 The *d*........................ has a large network of information.

5 This *s*........................ package is already selling well in the USA.

6.2 The meeting

1 At their meeting Klaus Jensen tells Anna Persson about the Fonex DB3. Before you listen, discuss in small groups:

1 the advantages of a home banking system.
2 the financial services suitable for a home banking service.

2 Now listen to Klaus Jensen's presentation. Make notes on what he tells Anna Persson about Excel's experience in Spain.

Note down:
1 the name of the Spanish bank.
2 how the Spanish project was set up.
3 how they attracted customers.
4 the range of services on offer.

3 When you make an informal presentation to a potential customer, you have to draw attention to the most important points. You may also need to refer to literature or visuals.

Listen to the dialogue again and note the phrases Klaus uses to:
1 introduce his presentation.
2 refer to the interactive system.
3 refer to the diagram.
4 offer to follow up his presentation.

6.3 Planning a presentation

Over to you 1 Now it's your turn to present a product. Here are the stages of an informal presentation to an individual or small group.

1 Introduce yourself.
2 State the aims of your presentation.
3 Tell your audience to stop you if they don't understand.
4 Present the product in clear stages. Refer to the written word, pictures and diagrams where necessary.
5 Sum up the presentation in one or two sentences.
6 Ask for questions.
7 Thank your audience.

2 Here is information about another of Excel's products. You have to present this product to a potential customer.

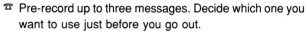

THE EXCEL PHONEMASTER

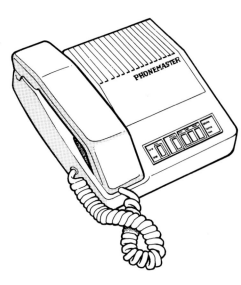

The intelligent telephone answering machine

Now you need never worry about being away from the office or your home. The EXCEL PHONEMASTER will take care of everything you can think of – and a few things you haven't thought of.

Just look at all these special features.

☎ Pre-record up to three messages. Decide which one you want to use just before you go out.
☎ 30-minute recording tape
☎ Hi-fi speaker for extra quality play-back
☎ Print-out of time/date of each recorded call
☎ Ring-in facility – you can call the machine from the airport, restaurant or wherever you are and listen to the messages recorded.
☎ Two-year warranty
☎ The intelligent telephone – if you can't get through to someone and you're going out, simply record a message on your PHONEMASTER and tap in the telephone number. The PHONEMASTER will call up every ten minutes until it gets through. The print out will show when the call was delivered. And of course the receiver of your call can leave a message on the PHONEMASTER as well!

For full technical details see page 6

THE FUTURE. HERE TODAY WITH EXCEL.

6.4 Talking about graphs

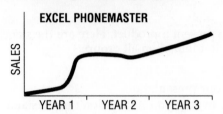

EXCEL PHONEMASTER

SALES

YEAR 1   YEAR 2   YEAR 3

1 Study this commentary on the Phonemaster sales graph.

At the beginning sales were very low, but after the advertising campaign, they increased sharply, then levelled off for about a year. Now sales are rising steadily and the Phonemaster is the fastest-selling product in this market sector.

2 Look at these two graphs about Excel products. Say how things changed during the period shown. Here's the vocabulary you need to talk about the graphs.

verbs	adverbs	adjectives
to increase	slightly	high
to rise	steadily	low
to level off	sharply	
to fall		

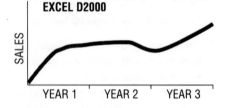

EXCEL D2000

SALES

YEAR 1   YEAR 2   YEAR 3

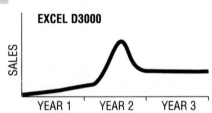

EXCEL D3000

SALES

YEAR 1   YEAR 2   YEAR 3

6.5 Klaus's report

1 Klaus Jensen has to make written reports of his meetings during his trip to Scandinavia. Fill in the form for his meeting with Anna Persson.

SALES TOUR REPORT

Location   *Svensaka Bank, Stockholm*   Purpose of meeting

Date   *15 May*............................   ....

Participants ....   Comments

....

....   Follow-up

....

2 Anna Persson dictated a short report on her meeting with Klaus Jensen. The report is for Nils Lundgren, Svensaka's Purchasing Manager.

Listen to Anna dictating the report.
1 She makes **three** important mistakes. Can you spot them?
2 What does she plan to do next week?
3 What does she suggest for the following week?

3 Here is Klaus Jensen's letter to Anna Persson following their meeting. Fill in the missing prepositions.

Dear Anna

Thank you very much .... seeing me last week.

As promised, I enclose a copy .... the documentation .... the home

banking system installed .... us .... Spain .... the Banco Comercial

.... Madrid. If you have any questions .... the technical data, please let

me know.

I am also sending you details .... a Communications Conference which

will be held here .... Frankfurt .... early October. I hope you will

decide to attend.

I will contact you again next week after you have had a chance to think

.... our proposals and to discuss them .... your colleagues.

Yours sincerely

Klaus Jensen

Klaus Jensen
Software Engineering (Sales)
Enc

---

4 Anna Persson discusses the Communications Conference with Nils Lundgren and decides to go. She writes to Klaus Jensen to tell him of her decision and to suggest another meeting.

Your task is to write Anna's letter. Here are some points to help you.

Thank you very much ...	(for what?)	*I have decided ...*	(what?)
Would it be possible ...?	(to do what? why?)		
Please let me know ...	(what?)		

6.5 The franchising game

1 A franchise is a licence to sell products and services under an established brand name. Worldwide franchises include Wimpy, PIP Printing, Kentucky Fried Chicken and Benetton.

Before you read a newspaper article about a successful franchising operation, think about the advantages and disadvantages of franchises for the franchiser (*the company giving the licence*) and the franchisee (*the individual paying for the licence*).

2 Now read the story of one successful franchise and answer the questions on the next page.

THE BODY SHOP – A NATURAL WINNER!

Juice of a cactus plant from New Mexico, cocoa butter from Tahiti, pineapple juice from Sri Lanka, flower oils from Japan. These are just a few of the exotic substances which go into a range of natural skin and hair care products sold all over the world. It all started in 1976 when the first Body Shop opened in Brighton, with the help of a $6,000 loan from a friendly bank manager. Now the chain comprises over 220 stores, exclusively selling its products in 23 countries. All but eight of the stores are owned by franchisees.

Anita Roddick, Managing Director of Body Shop International plc and one of the world's newest tycoons, admits that in the early days she didn't even know what franchising was!

The daughter of Italian immigrants, she taught history at a local secondary school, before going abroad to work first for the International Herald Tribune in their Paris library, then for the International Labour Office in Geneva where she organized seminars on women's rights.

On her travels, she developed an interest in local beauty customs and, along the way, got married. She and her husband returned to England and tried running the family restaurant, her first and, so far, only failure! That's when she decided to take a chance on the Body Shop.

There is now a worldwide network of stores in Europe, the Far East, Australia and Canada, with an annual turnover of $14.2 million. So far she has avoided the United States. 'It's Japan I'm after,' says Anita. 'That's the big challenge for us.'

What did Anita Roddick do:

1 in Geneva?   4 in Paris?
2 in Brighton?   5 on her travels?
3 in a local secondary school? 6 when she returned to England?

3 Here are some numbers from the text. What do they refer to?

1 14.2 million   3 1976   5 220
2 8   4 23   6 6,000

4 Find words in the text which mean:

1 a dynamic business person running a large company.
2 volume of business.
3 something difficult to do but worth trying.
4 money borrowed from a bank.

6.6 Anna Persson and Klaus Jensen in Frankfurt

Anna and Klaus are in a restaurant in Frankfurt. Their discussions are finished. Now they are relaxing. Klaus asks Anna how she started with Svensaka. Listen to their conversation and tick the correct answer.

✔

Anna studied *(physics/economics/music)* at *(Stockholm/Copenhagen/Uppsala)*.
She worked for her *(father/brother/husband)* in his *(banking/post office/ engineering)* business. Then she had a job in a *(post office/university/bank)*.
Finally, she got a job in the *(Engineering/International Exchange/Overseas Arrangements)* Department. She was there for $(2\frac{1}{2}/2\frac{1}{4}/3\frac{1}{2})$ *years)*. She found her present job in the Purchasing Department through *(a friend/her father/an advertisement)*.

6.7 On the spot

Now work with a partner. Find out everything you can about your partner's background *(education, training, experience)*.

Here are some notes to help you.

What/do/university/college/school?   *Why/leave?*
What/do/after that?   *How/get/present job?*

Language focus – Past tenses

1   We use the Past Simple to talk about events that happened at a specific time in the past.

*We **saw** the representative from your company last week.*
*They **installed** the new machine two weeks ago.*
***Did** you **visit** Svensaka during your trip to Sweden?*

2   The Past Continuous is used to establish the background to a past action.

*The economy **was beginning** to improve when we launched the product.*
*What **were** you **doing** when I telephoned?*
*I **was programming** the computer.*

Key words to use with the Past Continuous are **while** and **when**.

3   The Past Perfect (**had** + past participle) is used to describe an action which was already over when another past action took place.

*They **had** already **left** when we arrived.*
*When Anna entered university, she **had completed** four years study of English.*

Key words to use with the Past Perfect are **when, after, before** and **already.**

4   Look at this paragraph. Put the verb in brackets into the Past Continuous or Past Perfect .

Launching the product was not so simple. After we .... *(decide)* to go ahead, we asked a team of designers to come up with proposals. While we .... *(wait),* we did a complete market survey. When we .... *(analyze)* the results of the survey, we found that people .... *(look)* for a slightly different product, so we had to tell the design people what we .... *(find).* The problem was that they .... *(already do)* the basic design. In the end everything was sorted out, thank goodness!

5   Write a CV (*curriculum vitae*) giving details of your education, training and work experience. Make a list of all the facts first, then write a short paragraph giving more details.

UNIT 7 *All work and no play*

In this unit you will:

- describe an industrial process.
- discuss sports and free time activities.
- read about quality control.
- take and give a telephone order.

7.1 A tour of the factory

1 Klaus Jensen is taking Anna Persson round the Excel factory outside Frankfurt and showing her how the Excel Phonemaster, the telephone answering machine, is assembled. Listen to their conversation and answer these questions.

1 Where are some of the parts imported from?
2 What problem does the Purchasing Department have?
3 How many different systems are produced here?
4 What happens in the Finishing Department?

2 Listen again to the conversation and put in the missing verbs.

1 Most of the work is .... by NC machines.

2 All the switching systems are .... here.

3 Of course, some of the parts can be .... in Taiwan more cheaply.

4 They're .... and then all the components are .... here.

5 That's the Finishing Department where everything's ....

6 Then a registration number is .... onto each piece of equipment and the Excel logo is .... on.

7 And then the goods go out to Dispatch, through that door, where they're .... out to customers all over the world.

45

3 Underline the stressed syllable in these words.

1 registration	5 assembled	9 environment
2 circuit	6 dispatch	10 equipment
3 logo	7 numerically	11 customers
4 electronics	8 similar	12 business

4 You are going to give your partner information about a production process. Before you start, check in the *Language focus* section that you know how to use the Passive correctly.

Student A Look at the information about the Camcorder and be ready to tell your partner about it.

Student B Look at the information about kitchen furniture on page 134 and be ready to tell your partner about it.

THE CAMCORDER

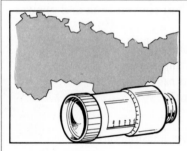

LENS MADE IN
CZECHOSLOVAKIA

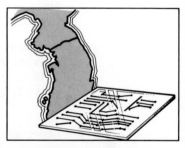

ELECTRONIC CONTROL
SYSTEM IMPORTED FROM
SOUTH KOREA

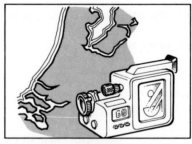

ASSEMBLED IN HOLLAND

PACKAGED AND DISTRIBUTED
FROM WAREHOUSE IN
HOLLAND

7.2 Quality control

1 Before you read the Excel advertisement, discuss in groups these points. Do you agree or disagree?

● Quality is more important than price.
● 100% reliability is impossible.

2 Now read the advertisement. Find the facts which show it is true Excel has a reputation second to none for high quality and reliability.

A Tenfold Increase in Product Quality Every Ten Years. Is it possible?

It certainly is. We've made it a worldwide company goal. It's part of a long-term programme which will help us to compete with electronics suppliers from every part of the world.

Many of our products are now 'certified' by our customers. A 'certified' product means that it is of such high quality that the purchaser does not have to inspect shipments when they arrive at the factory.

In France, our ignition systems are certified by two of France's leading car manufacturers.

In Germany we asked our customers recently what they thought of our two-way radios. The answer came back loud and clear: 99.74% reported that they were completely satisfied.

In Livingstone in Scotland we produce semiconductors. The high level of quality has improved by a factor of ten in the last four years. And we now have customers who register zero defects at their incoming inspection.

All in all, Excel has a reputation second to none for high quality and reliability in the electronics field.

THE FUTURE. HERE TODAY WITH EXCEL.

---

3 The words **it** and **they** appear frequently in the text. Underline each example and then decide what they refer to.

Example: *In Germany we asked our customers recently what **they** thought of our two-way radios.*

They refers to our customers.

4   Underline the correct word in these sentences.

1   Excel has a reputation/reliability for high quality products.
2   We want to complete/compete with electronics suppliers worldwide.
3   Our consumers/customers are 100% satisfied with the product.
4   The customer does not have to inspect shippings/shipments.
5   We product/produce high quality goods.
6   Reliability is very important in the field of electronics/electronic.

7.3   The Sports Centre

 1   Listen to Klaus Jensen showing Anna Persson round the Excel Sports Centre and answer these questions.

1   Which of these sports can Excel employees do at the Centre?
2   What other activities are available at the Centre?
3   Who paid for the Centre?
4   What sports does Klaus play?

2   Work in pairs. Ask your partner:

● how he or she keeps fit.
● which sports he or she enjoys playing.
● which sports he or she enjoys watching.

● Tell the rest of the class what you have found out about your partner.

7.4   Extending the Sports Centre

1   The company has had a successful year and has decided to give $60,000 to improve the Sports Centre. Look at the plan of the Centre and decide what to do with the money. Make sure that your plan offers good value for money and will be popular with the members of the Centre. Work in pairs or small groups.

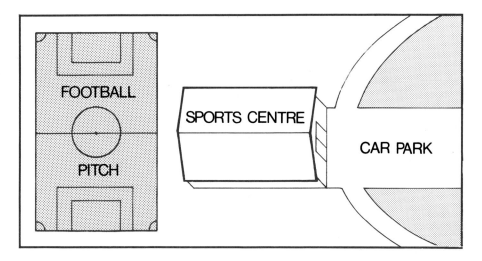

Here are some of the ideas members of the Centre have had.

1 Build a new squash court ($50,000).
2 Construct two outdoor tennis courts ($20,000).
3 Install Jacuzzis in the fitness room ($16,000).
4 Buy floodlighting for the football pitch ($30,000).
5 Build a drinks bar and lounge ($58,000).
6 Lay out a running track ($30,000).

The Sports Committee sent out a questionnaire to all members. Here are some of the results.

Top priority (Total 100%)		Would be useful/popular (Members could name more than one item, so total is more than 100%)
1	24%	33%
2	12%	24%
3	6%	20%
4	19%	52%
5	29%	71%
6	10%	18%

Here are some phrases which will help you put forward your ideas to the group:

I think the ... is the best choice because ...
In my view the ... would be very popular because ...
We don't need a ... because ...
Yes, that's a good idea, but/because ...
I disagree with you about the ... because ...

2 When you have reached a decision, write a memo to the Chairman of the Sports Committee giving your ideas.

7.5 On the spot – taking a telephone message

 1 You are in the Sales Office one day when the phone rings. It's an order from a company in Scotland. Quickly you pick up an order form and start taking down details.

Date 4th June   **Time** 15. 40

Company   **Contact name**

                                                      Contact phone

Quantity   **Reference**   **Description**

Delivery

Invoicing/payment

Comments

---

2 You pick up the phone in your office, but the call is not for you. You make quick notes. Pass on the message to a colleague in the Sales Department. Work in pairs.

Student B   Go to page 135.

Student A   Give this order over the phone to Student B in the Sales Department.

Company ESTORIL S. A.   **Contact name** FERNANDO

                                         Contact phone EXTENSION 2011

Quantity   **Reference**   **Description**
  20   89/FR/2413   Microphones
  25   89/FG/9807   Loudspeakers

Delivery As soon as possible to :
              ESTORIL, Barcelona, Spain

Invoicing/payment As usual 60 days credit .

Comments Please send 10 copies of your brochure in Spanish

Language focus – the Passive

1 To make the Passive, just take the correct tense of the verb **to be** and add the past participle, e.g *was done*.

We use the Passive:

1 When the object of the sentence is more important than the real subject, e.g. *50,000 cars **are produced** in Oxford every three months.*
2 When you don't know the real subject or you don't want to show that you know it, e.g. *My wallet **was stolen** yesterday. (I don't know who stole it.)* or *The equipment **was damaged** during the testing period. (I don't want to say who damaged it.)*
3 We can use the Passive with all the modal and auxiliary verbs (*can, should, may, must, will, have*). Add **be** + the past participle to the modal or auxiliary. Here are three examples:
*All doors **must be closed.***
The goods **can be delivered** tomorrow.
*We hope you **will be impressed** with our service.*

2 Put the verbs in brackets into the Passive.

1 The order .... (*place*) ten days ago.

2 The goods .... (*deliver*) yesterday.

3 The brochure .... (*print*) in English and French every year.

4 You .... (*will inform*) when the order is ready.

5 The Fonex .... (*may launch*) in the USA soon.

6 Discounts .... (*give*) to all regular customers.

7 The message .... (*take*) by my colleague at 2.00pm.

8 The goods .... (*can supply*) by our company in Spain.

3 Change these sentences into the Passive if you think there is a good reason for doing so. Discuss with a partner how the meaning changes, if at all.

1 They make 12,000 PCBs every month at the factory in Livingstone.
2 The telex operator sent the telex at 16.35 yesterday.
3 The customer received the goods two days late.
4 The engineer services the fax machine once a year.
5 Signor Bellati wrote the report himself.

UNIT 8 *Things have changed*

In this unit you will:

- discuss sales figures.
- make arrangements for a European tour.
- invite a colleague to a social occasion.
- read about the most expensive cities in the world.

8.1 Report to the USA

1 Miguel García is the Manager of Excel Spain, Excel's sales and distribution company in Madrid. He has to inform both the Head Office of Excel Europe in Lyon and the Excel Corporation in Boston Massachusetts about his activities.

Listen to him talking on the telephone to Harold Goodman in Boston and fill in the gaps in the table below for June. What is the missing product code?

"Fine, how are things with you?"

PRODUCT CODE	SALES MAY	JUNE	JULY	AUGUST
PD 14	$20,000	....	....	....
PD 15	$18,000	....	....	....
PD 16	$7,500	....	....	....
....	$50,000	....	....	....
TOTAL SALES VALUE (this year)	$95,500	....	....	....
TOTAL SALES VALUE (last year)	....	....	....	....

52

2 Now you have the information about the June figures, fill in the information in Miguel's monthly report for June.

MONTHLY SALES REPORT : JUNE 19—

The most important development this month has been the increase in sales of the .... system by 50%. The new customer, Benefin SA, has said it will purchase $25,000 worth every month for the next two years.

Other changes are small. Sales of the .... have increased by $1,000 but sales of the .... have fallen by $250. Sales of the .... have remained steady at $18,000.

We are running a new sales campaign at the moment and hope that there will be a general improvement in the figures next month.

3 Look at these examples of how to say numbers correctly.

4,579: *four thousand, five hundred and seventy-nine* **(BrE)**
four thousand, five hundred, seventy-nine **(AmE)**
3.5: *three point five*
$5.65: *five dollars (and) sixty-five cents*
$6\frac{1}{2}$: *six and a half*
35%: *thirty-five per cent*

● Now practise saying these numbers.

1 20,875
2 0.5
3 $3\frac{1}{2}$
4 689
5 14.75
6 43%
7 1m 80 cm
8 $2\frac{1}{4}$ hours
9 $1.5 million
10 2.75 DM

4 The PD14 and PD15 have different specifications. Can you find the differences? Work in pairs.

Student B Go to page 135.
Student A Describe the PD14.

PD14 SPECIFICATION
Size: 16 cm x 14.5 cm x 2.5 cm
Power: 220-240 volts
Speed: 185 operations per second
Working life: 3 years
Working temperatures: 10-35 degrees Centigrade
Price: 2,300 FF

8.2   Phone calls in July and August

1   In July and August Miguel García calls Harold Goodman in Boston again. Work in pairs.

Student A   You are Harold. Ask Miguel for his July figures. Note them down on the table on page 135. Ask him to explain the results.

Student B   You are Miguel. Go to page 135 for the information.

Change roles.

Student B   You are Harold. Ask Miguel for the August figures. Note them down on the table on page 135. Ask him to explain the results.

Student A   You are Miguel. Go to page 135 for the information.

2   Why have things changed? Harold Goodman is not happy with Excel Spain's performance. He compares last year's figures for May-August with this year's figures.

First, add up the total sales value for each of the months this year. Then listen to Miguel and Harold discussing the figures. Note last year's figures down on the table on page 52. What reasons does Miguel give for the changes? Decide which of the explanations you accept and which you do not accept.

8.3   Visitors from the States

1   Once a year, a group of top American managers come over to Europe from the States. They want to make sure that everything is running smoothly in the European operation.

This visit is very important for all the European Excel companies. When the Americans go back, they decide on the investment for the coming year. They will invest more money in the Excel companies which they think are doing well.

Miguel García is responsible for the Americans' visit to Spain. Here is the timetable he has arranged.

Mon 18 Sept	Arrive Madrid Airport.
	Car to Excel Spain offices.
	Meet admin. staff.
	Dinner with senior local management.
Tue 19 Sept	Meeting at Excel offices to review Excel Spain SA's past year.
	Lunch in central Madrid.
	Visit to Benefin SA (JCAL customer).
	Dinner with senior staff.
Wed 20 Sept	Depart from Madrid Airport for Lyon.

Miguel sent the programme to Harold Goodman in Boston two weeks ago. Today he received this fax. List the changes which Harold Goodman proposes.

```
Attention Miguel Garcia


Re  itinerary for visit to Spain

Arrival date now Tues 19 Sept Flight IB 234

arriving Madrid 18.40.  Please arrange visit to Benefin

Wednesday a.m. and meeting at your office Wednesday

p.m.  Flight Madrid - Lyon Thursday morning

Thanks and regards

Harold Goodman
```

Over to you **2** Now work in groups. You have three tasks.

Task 1

You must telephone Benefin to tell them about the change of plan. It is late in the afternoon and no one is in the office. Record a message on their telephone answering machine explaining the situation. Apologize for the change in plans and ask if the time of the visit can be changed. Start like this: *I'm ringing from Excel. It's about ...*

Task 2

Write a memo to your colleagues telling them that the date and time of the review meeting has changed. Don't forget to set out the memo correctly.

Task 3

Write a fax to Harold Goodman confirming that you have made all the necessary changes.

8.4 An expensive place to stay

1 Read this article about the cost of living around the world and note down information about the following cities:

1 Bombay   5 Jeddah
2 Zurich   6 Rio de Janeiro
3 Abu Dhabi   7 London
4 Lagos

AROUND THE WORLD

Lagos is the most expensive city in the world for the business tourist - and that's official. This surprising piece of information is included in a survey for business travellers of all the major cities of the world. It was prepared by the Union Bank of Switzerland.

For the past year they have been collecting information about rent, hotel and restaurant prices, wages and salaries.

The most expensive cities to live in are, according to the survey, Lagos, Tokyo, New York and Abu Dhabi. The cheapest cities to visit are Lisbon, Rio de Janeiro, Istanbul and Bangkok. The pay is worst in Jakarta, Manila and Bombay. It's best in Switzerland (Zurich, Basel and Geneva), Canada and the United States.

Visitors to London often complain about the high hotel prices. But in the last few years, hotel prices in other cities have become even more expensive. It now costs even more to spend a night in a hotel in Istanbul, Chicago, Jeddah or São Paulo.

Lagos is the most expensive city in the world

2 Discuss these questions in pairs or small groups.

● Have you visited any of the cities mentioned in the article?
● Where is the cheapest/most expensive place you have visited?
● Which is the most expensive town/city in your country?

8.5 On the spot 1

You are a senior employee of Excel Spain. Albert Gomez is one of the Americans coming over next month. When you were over in the States two years ago, Albert invited you and your wife to dinner. Now you want to return his hospitality and invite him and his wife to dinner at your house on the evening of Wednesday 20 September.

Here is the letter Albert sent you two years ago. Use it as the basis for your letter of invitation.

339 Peachtree Boulevard
Lambino Heights
BOSTON
Mass. 20940

Dear Jorge,

I am very glad to hear that you are coming over to Boston next month. I look forward to meeting you on 15 November at our main offices here in Boston.

I know you will be very busy during your short stay, but I hope you will have enough time to visit my wife and me here at our home. We would like to invite you and your wife to dinner, if possible on 16 or 17 November.

We can arrange to pick you up in our car and take you back to your hotel afterwards.

I do hope you will accept and look forward to hearing from you soon.

Have a good trip!

With best wishes,
sincerely yours,
Albert Gomez

8.6 On the spot 2

You are Miguel García. You have just shown the American group round the Excel Spain offices. Now it's lunchtime and you are in a restaurant. Your partner is Felix Kramer from Boston. What would you say in these social situations?

1 You want to offer Felix a drink. Suggest the local red wine.
2 You want to offer Felix the menu. Recommend the *merluza,* a popular Spanish fish.
3 Ask Felix about his job with Excel in Boston.
4 Ask him about his family in Boston. You know he has a wife and two children.
5 Ask him how he spends his free time. You've heard that his hobby is ballooning!

Language focus – the Present Perfect

1   We use the Present Perfect to describe an event in the past which has a connection with the present. Sometimes there is a time phrase which shows this clearly, e.g. *this week, today, so far, already, just, until now, this year, yet.*

Here are two examples.

I**'ve sent** them three telexes this week and they **haven't answered** them **yet.**

So far **we've received** *three enquiries about the PD 34.*

Sometimes it is clear that the result of a past action is very important for the present.

*I've **lost** my glasses. (I can't see without them.)*
*I'm afraid I've **forgotten** your name. (Please remind me.)*
*We've **sent** the engineer to Abu Dhabi. (He's there at the moment.)*

In other cases, the past time is not specific, so we use the Present Perfect.

Have *you* **met** *Albert Gomez? (In your professional life until now)*
Have *you ever* **been** *to Thailand? (In your life until now)*
Felix Kramer **has been** *a great success in this job. (He's still in the job.)*

2   Use the Present Perfect in these sentences.

1 We .... (*already send*) the engineer a telex.

2 So far we .... (*not hear*) from the customer.

3 .... (*you ever visit*) Indonesia?

4 I .... (*lose*) all my traveller's cheques. Can you lend me some money?

5 We .... (*just print*) the catalogues in English.

6 The engineer .... (*test*) the components and cannot find anything wrong.

3   Are you dynamic? Try this quiz. Which of the following have you done in the last twelve months? Fill in YES or NO for yourself first. Then ask a partner.

Have you in the last six months...	YOU	PARTNER
visited a foreign country?		
taken up a new job?		
attended a training course?		
asked for an increase in your salary?		
taken up a new hobby or pastime?		
made new friends?		
learned a foreign language?		
started a fitness training programme?		
taken on more responsibility a) at work? b) in your home life?		

Give one point for each YES answer. See page 136 for a not very serious guide to your personality when you have finished.

4 **Been** and **gone.** Look at this dialogue.

Alberto Hello Dulce. Can I have a word with Miguel, please?
Dulce I'm afraid he's not here.
Alberto Where's he gone?
Dulce I really don't know. I'm expecting him back any minute.
Miguel comes in.
Miguel Hello, Alberto. How are you?
Alberto: Miguel, I've been looking for you everywhere. Where have you been?

    1 *Where's Miguel **gone**?*
    2 *Where's Miguel **been**?*
Can you work out the difference in meaning between these two sentences?

5 Put **been** or **gone** into these sentences.

    1 I'm sorry, Miguel's not here this week. He's .... to Abu Dhabi.

    2 Hello, Miguel. Did you have a good trip? Where have you .... ?

    3 You're very late for this meeting. Where have you .... ?

    4 Mr García can't attend the meeting. He's .... to Paris.

    5 I've never .... to Bangkok, so I'm looking forward to this trip.

In this unit you will:

- find out about Excel's latest product.
- deal with a customer's problem.
- read an article about company image.
- carry out a negotiation between supplier and customer.

9.1 The RTDS

1 Excel has recently developed a new system of networking data on large sites such as oil refineries. Here are diagrams of the old system and the new system.

1 What changes has Excel made in the system of transmitting data?
2 What do you think are the advantages of the new system?
3 Do you see any disadvantages?

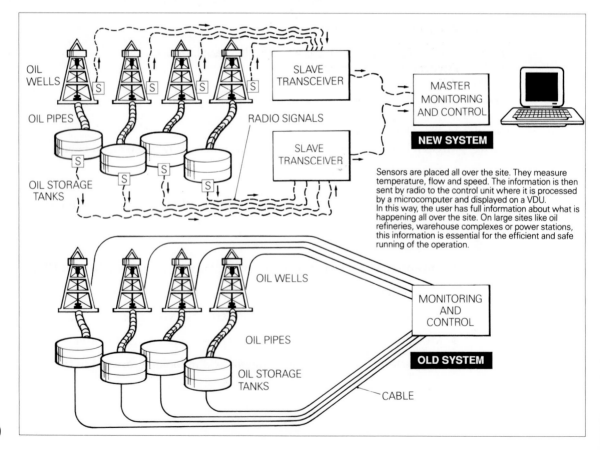

Sensors are placed all over the site. They measure temperature, flow and speed. The information is then sent by radio to the control unit where it is processed by a microcomputer and displayed on a VDU.
In this way, the user has full information about what is happening all over the site. On large sites like oil refineries, warehouse complexes or power stations, this information is essential for the efficient and safe running of the operation.

2 Complete these sentences using information from the text and diagrams.

1 The sensors measure.. .

2 Information is displayed ....

3 The RTDS is suitable for sites such as ....

4 The information is sent by radio to ....

5 Excel have made changes in the system of ....

6 The sensors are placed ....

9.2 A call from the Middle East

1 Chantal Girard is at the Excel Europe office in Lyon. She works in Customer Support Services. Every day she receives calls, faxes and telexes from Excel customers. Sometimes they are having problems with Excel equipment. Sometimes they need help or advice on how to operate the equipment correctly.

Monday morning's call is from the Middle East. Listen and note down the essential information.

2 The next day Chantal listens to the messages on her telephone answering machine. The most urgent message is from Mr Alamuddin.

1 What's the problem?
2 What does Mr Alamuddin want?

3 Before Chantal can decide what to do, she receives this fax from the engineer. Read the fax and find out:

1 why the engineer hasn't contacted Chantal before.
2 when he will arrive at MidEast Oil.
3 what he wants Mr Alamuddin to do before his visit.

```
To Excel Lyon
For the attention of Chantal Girard, Customer Support Services


Service visit to MidEast oil, Mr Alamuddin


Regret delay in contacting you.  Site had telex and
fax facilities down for 12 hours.  Job now completed.
Will arrive MidEast tomorrow (Wednesday) afternoon.
Please ask Mr Alamuddin to prepare list of problems
with RTDS.  Also make an appointment for me to see
MidEast chief site engineer.


Thanks  Michael Braun
```

4   Work in pairs.

Student A   You are Chantal Girard.
Call Mr Alamuddin.
Apologize for the delay and tell him the reason.
Tell him the service engineer's name and when he will arrive.
Give him the two messages from the service engineer.

Student B   You are Mr Alamuddin.
Accept Ms Girard's apology.
Note the messages from the service engineer.
Tell Ms Girard you hope there will be no further delay.

5   Now send a telex or fax to the engineer, Braun.

- Reconfirm arrangements for his visit to MidEast Oil.
- Tell him you have given Mr Alamuddin the messages.
- Ask him to contact you when he has finished the repairs at MidEast.

9.3   Who pays?

1   The engineer completes his repairs to the RTDS in three days. Mr Alamuddin is delighted when the government inspector finds that everything is in order at the refinery. But who pays for the repairs? Read this extract from the Service Contract and find this piece of information. Remember that the system was installed less than a year ago.

2.1 For a period of two years from installation, the control system is covered by a full guarantee. During the period of the guarantee all repairs to the system are free (including parts, labour). Excel will bear the cost of travel of the engineer to the site.

2.2 A routine service check will be made after three months, thereafter annually. There will be a fixed charge of $500 dollars per inspection, plus reasonable hotel and travel charges incurred locally.

---

2   Three weeks later Mr Alamuddin receives this bill from Excel.

EXCEL

EXCEL EUROPE

INVOICE No. 1096   Date: 16 November 19—

In account with MidEast Oil
Attention: Mr Alamuddin

Repair of RTDS system : 21-23 October 19—
Hotel bills (receipts attached) $876.00
Local travel expenses $108.50
                                       $984.50

Signed .... *Chantal Girard* ....

Mr Alamuddin does not feel he should have to pay the bill so he calls Excel. Work in pairs and negotiate an agreement on the telephone as Mr Alamuddin and Chantal Girard.

9.4 How to improve your image

1 Before you read this article from a business magazine, discuss these questions with a partner or in small groups.

- What problems have you had when telephoning large companies?
- Can you describe the ideal reception area?

2 Now read the article.

1 Note down all the things mentioned in the article which can create a bad impression about a company.
2 Note down all the things mentioned in the article which can create a good impression.

FIRST IMPRESSIONS COUNT

Would you like to do business with a company that takes 30 seconds to answer the telephone, then lets you hang on and on while they look for the person you want, or puts you through to an extension without telling you that they are away for the day?

Not really. If they can't train their telephone operators, the chances are they don't make very good products. That's what the potential customer will think because first impressions count.

Successful companies know that you have to look after all aspects of your business, not just the technical and production side. IBM, featured in Peter's and Waterman's *In Search of Excellence*, have standard procedures for dealing with incoming calls. After an opening greeting, the operator transfers the caller to the extension and tells him that it's ringing. If there is no answer within 30 seconds, the

caller is asked if anyone else can help or if they can take a message. Even temporary operators follow this procedure.

What about that pile of computer paper, delivered over a week ago, that's still sitting in the reception area? Wally Olins, Chief Executive of Wolff Olins, one of Europe's top design firms, talks of the importance of the 'journey' a visitor makes through your company. It's not only untidy offices that create a bad impression. People eating snacks at their desks, reading, doing crossword puzzles or knitting all have the same effect - that's why they are all banned by IBM during working hours.

Sociologist Sheena Wilson was asked by Herman Miller, the big American furniture manufacturers, to produce a survey showing how successful companies manage their facilities. In Company X she was kept waiting in a cold gatehouse full of stale cigarette smoke, then taken to a badly decorated lobby with uncomfortable chairs and old magazines. In Company Y she was given a list of the people she would be seeing, offered fresh coffee in a proper cup and taken to a sitting area with good modern chairs, the latest corporate literature and current magazines. Guess which company was producing better results!

The lesson is that if you want to put excellence into place, start out with the way your office looks. It's the most effective way of telling people what you want them to believe about your company.

3 Fill in the missing prepositions in these phrases taken from the text.

1 Would you like to do business .... a company ...

2 ... then lets you hang .... and ....

3 ... if you want to put excellence .... place ...

4 If there is no answer .... 30 seconds ...

5 ... the operator transfers the caller .... the extension ...

6 ... or put you .... to an extension ...

7 ... then taken .... a badly decorated lobby ....
uncomfortable chairs ...

8 ... people eating snacks .... their desks ...

"Good afternoon. Kelly, Henderson & Farnsworth."

9.5   On the spot – apologizing

1 When things go wrong, it often isn't enough just to say 'Sorry!' You also
have to give an explanation. Look at these two lists of apologies and
explanations.

Match the apology to the explanation.

Apologies

1 I'm sorry I'm so late.
2 I'm sorry I forgot the appointment.
3 I'm afraid the report won't be ready on time.
4 I apologize for the delay in delivery.
5 I'm terribly sorry about all the typing errors.
6 I'm afraid I can't come to the meeting tomorrow.

Explanations

A I need more statistics from the Frankfurt office.
B My diary was stolen.
C I have to show visitors from Japan round the factory.
D Our temporary secretary sent it off before I could check it.
E We had problems at the factory.
F I had to deal with a complaint from our most important customer.

2 What would you say in these situations? Think of a good excuse which will explain why things went wrong.

1 A customer is on the phone. He ordered 100 PC boards and he has received 1000 from you.
2 This afternoon the Planning Committee is meeting in your office. At 11.00 a colleague calls you to say she hasn't received the agenda, which you promised to send her last week.
3 The Financial Controller in the USA calls you up to complain that your monthly figures are always late.
4 The Office Manager complains to you that deliveries to your department are often left at Reception for several days.

Language focus – Past Simple or Present Perfect?

In Unit 6 we looked at the Past Simple, in Unit 8 the Present Perfect. Don't forget the basic difference between these two tenses.

In sentences with the Past Simple we are talking or writing about a specific time in the past, e.g. *yesterday, three days ago, in 1981.*

In sentences with the Present Perfect, the action may be finished or may continue into the present, but the time stated is not finished, e.g. *until now, since 1981, so far,* or is not stated at all.

Fill in the gaps in this short presentation. Put the verb in brackets into the Past Simple or Present Perfect.

'I'd like to report on the installation of the new computer system. We hope everything will be completed by the end of next month. Two of my colleagues .... (1) (*attend*) training sessions and the suppliers .... (2) (*visit*) us at least six times over the last three months. We .... (3) (*receive*) the hardware last week and the programming will all be done in the next four to six weeks. The manufacturers .... (4) (*tell*) me on the phone yesterday that they .... (5) (*send*) off all the manuals to us.

I .... (6) (*already write*) a report on the differences between the new system and the old one. As you know, I .... (7) (*feel*) for a long time that our computer facility is not adequate. Now, I think, we've got it right. Bob, you .... (8) (*ask*) me a few days ago to report on the details of the new system. I .... (9) (*not have*) a lot of time to think about it, but these are the main points ... '

Macdonald Harris News

Macdonald Harris has its own in-house newspaper. Here is a selection of articles from this month's edition. Read them and answer the questions.

EXCEL SUCCEEDS IN TAKEOVER BID FOR DREXEL SCHUMANN

It was announced last week that Excel Europe has successfully completed the takeover of Drexel Schumann, the fast-growing West German software house. The bid was accepted by Drexel's board of directors in the face of strong competition from other major European companies.

Excel Europe has moved from fifth to third place this year in the European market for systems engineering. This position was consolidated recently when the company won a substantial contract with the newspaper and magazine group INC to supply them with systems for their new national distribution centre outside Aachen. This is planned to be the most advanced warehouse of its type in Europe.

Excel Europe has already shown that it can supply the most appropriate selection of hardware, packages and application software to meet customers' requirements. The purchase of a company like Drexel Schumann with all its skills and expertise can help the group to become Europe's number one in the very near future.

1 Which of these statements is correct?
   a) Excel has won a contract with a computer services firm.
   b) Excel has supplied equipment to a computer services firm.
   c) Excel has bought a computer services firm.

2 Which company plans to have a new national distribution centre?
   a) Excel Europe.
   b) INC.
   c) Drexel Schumann.

3 What is Excel's current position in the European market for systems engineering?
   a) Number three.
   b) Number five.
   c) Number one.

4 What word or phrase is used to mean:
   a) an offer?
   b) made stronger, more solid?
   c) larger, worth a lot of money?
   d) a large building for storing things?
   e) suitable or correct in a particular situation?
   f) the buying of something?

MACDONALD HARRIS VOTES FOR SMOKING BAN

A complete ban on smoking may soon be introduced after the results of a questionnaire sent to all employees in the company showed that just over three out of four employees agree with a proposal to ban the habit at work.

If the ban goes ahead, then smoking, already forbidden in the factory, will no longer be allowed in the offices or in the canteen and reception areas.

The results of the questionnaire are in line with a recent survey published last November which showed that of Britain's top 1,000 companies around a half had either a voluntary or formal agreement on no-smoking areas. Another quarter were either considering a no-smoking policy or intended to do so in the next two or three years.

Already almost two thirds of companies in Britain have imposed some restrictions on employees smoking. In one company a boss has given smokers a room of their own - but with no furniture!

Smokers are facing more pressure than ever before to give up for both health and social reasons; it may not be long before there is a no-smoking clause in the majority of company contracts.

1 Which facts mentioned in the article do these percentages refer to?
   a) 76%   c) 53%
   b) 63%   d) 25%

2 Are the following sentences **true** or **false**?
   a) Smoking has been banned in all areas of Macdonald Harris.
   b) The majority of Macdonald Harris employees agree with a ban.
   c) There is a no-smoking clause in the majority of company contracts.

3 For discussion:
   Is there a ban on smoking in your company?
   Do you agree with this statement?
   I am against the introduction of a no-smoking clause in company contracts. Smokers must be allowed to decide for themselves when and if they want to give up the habit.'

PRODUCTION NEWS

210 production workers have voted to transfer to working four longer shifts to allow for increased production. The result of the vote backs a management plan to increase the length of their shifts from $7\frac{3}{4}$ hours to $9\frac{3}{4}$ hours. The company will take on more workers to cover the 'fifth day'.

The plan, which will start in the autumn, was put forward as an alternative to double shift working. It is seen as a means of raising production capacity by a limited amount rather than doubling it through the introduction of a night shift.

The company wants to raise production because of the increase in size of the Australasian market.

In an area where there is a 17% unemployment rate, the news is very welcome.

1 210 workers have voted
   a) to lengthen their shifts.
   b) to work night shifts.

2 The plan will mean
   a) production capacity goes up 100%.
   b) production capacity goes up less than 100%.

3 Read the article again and complete this sentence with one of the explanations.
   The plan was put forward because
   a) there is high unemployment in the area.
   b) the workers prefer day shifts to night shifts.
   c) a limited increase in production capacity is needed.
   d) the company needed more workers.

NEW SECURITY SYSTEMS

FOLLOWING A SERIES OF thefts, security has been increased. All of us, including the Managing Director, now have to wear an identity tag, complete with personal photograph. Visitors are given name badges with a code to indicate who in the company is responsible for them during their stay. Tags and badges must be clearly visible at all times. In addition, video phones have been installed at all points of entry to the building.

In recent weeks over £40,000 worth of electrical or electronic items have been stolen including £12,000 of video and closed circuit TV equipment from the training centre, also two desktop computers. And it doesn't stop there - just last month a set of golf clubs was taken from the reception area!

Security officer, Andrew Johnson, says that almost all the thefts have happened during normal working hours. The thieves can often be mistaken for visitors. For example, the computers were stolen by two well-dressed young men in their twenties who apparently walked in through the main door of the building, went up to the first floor and took the computers which were standing in a corridor waiting to be unpacked. They walked out again with them without anyone noticing.

All staff are asked to cooperate with the new systems; it's a small inconvenience to pay if we are to stop these thefts. Next time it could be *your* golf clubs!

1 Why has security been increased at Livingstone?
2 Note down the three new security systems introduced into the company.
3 Are these statements **true** or **false**?
   a) Most thefts happen after normal working hours.
   b) The thieves often look like visitors.
   c) The thieves only steal electrical or electronic equipment.

4 For discussion:
   Tell each other about the general security systems in your company or organization.
   Do you think they work well?
   Are the systems inconvenient for you, or for visitors?

LIONS HEADING FOR PROMOTION

With five wins out of their last five games, the Livingstone Lions are now only three points behind the leaders in the Second Division of the Scottish Conference League. They started the season as favourites, but surprised everyone by losing their first two matches.

'The team had a lot of new players,' explained captain Andy Mackenzie, 'and it took us a little while to begin playing well together.'

With two games still to play - one more than the current leaders Scottish Steel Limited - the Lions look sure of victory and promotion next season into the Premier Division.

1 Are the Livingstone Lions the current leaders of their division?
2 Did they begin the season well?
3 Have they got one or two more games still to play this season?

Here are two items of news about staff at Macdonald Harris. There is no punctuation. Read the items and then rewrite them putting in the punctuation marks and the capital letters.

Staff news

mrs elizabeth starr has been appointed financial controller after three years with the company in place of mr malcolm gray whose retirement was announced last month elizabeth has just returned from four weeks at corporate headquarters in boston which she says was a very valuable experience it is good to see women at the top in excel and lets hope elizabeth is the first of many

congratulations to alan jarvis of our research and development centre alan was chosen from 30 candidates to attend a six month management programme at harvard business school usa earlier this year he has successfully completed the course which he says was the hardest six months to date in his life

Personal reading activity

Choose an article or story which interests you in an English language magazine or newspaper and:

- write down the title or headline.
- read the article **quickly**. What is the subject of the article?
- read the article again. Choose five words or phrases which are new to you and make a note of them. Look them up in your dictionary and write down their meaning.

MANKOFF

"You're fired! Read all about it!"

UNIT 11 *Just sign here*

In this unit you will:

- study the language of contracts.
- negotiate the details of a contract.
- read about an expensive accident.
- write a fax message.

11.1 A new agent in Chicago

1 The Excel Corporation has decided to change its agent in the Chicago area. Bold Elextro has agreed in principle to become the agent there for Excel. Representatives of the two companies have already met once. The two sides now need a second meeting to finalize the details and draw up a contract.

Study the agenda for the meeting.

Meeting to discuss agency agreement between Excel Corporation and Bold Elextro
To be held at Excel Head Office on Thursday 15 October.

AGENDA

1. Overheads: who will pay the cost of the extra staff, office space, telephone/telex/fax?
2. Publicity material: how will we arrange this and who will bear the costs?
3. Technical back-up and sales training: levels of Excel investment.
4. Commission: rates and payment procedures.
5. Procedures for dealing with orders and deliveries.

---

2 What is/are:

1 overheads?
2 commission?
3 back-up?
4 publicity material?

5 sales training?
6 payment procedures?
7 investment?

With a partner, work out definitions for these terms. Use a dictionary if necessary.

70

3 Look at these extracts from a standard contract. Match each paragraph with one of the points on the agenda.

Agenda point	Standard contract
	All administrative costs will be paid by the Principal.
	The Agent will receive payments to the total value of 5% of all sales, payable annually in arrears.
	Advertising and promotional material will be supplied in reasonable quantities by the Principal.
	Goods will be delivered to the Agent within 28 (twenty-eight) days of the official order being received by the Principal.
	The Principal undertakes to provide all necessary training of the Agent's employees to enable them to promote the goods and/or services effectively.

4 Look at these words and phrases from the contract. Decide what they mean.

1 *annually*   means   a) every month.
                          b) every year.
                          c) every season.
2 *undertakes*   means   a) promises.
                          b) tries.
                          c) arranges.
3 *administrative* means   a) business.
                          b) official.
                          c) office.
4 *in arrears*   means   a) afterwards.
                          b) immediately.
                          c) in advance.
5 *Principal*   means   a) director.
                          b) seller.
                          c) lawyer.
6 *promote*   means   a) improve.
                          b) advertise and sell.
                          c) organize and arrange.

11.2 Discussing the details

1 Harold Goodman of Excel meets Markus Bold and Karen Klein of Bold Elextro to discuss the points on the agenda. Listen to their discussion and note down what the two sides agree about:

1 the number of old brochures Excel will provide.
2 the number of new brochures Excel will provide.
3 printing Bold Elextro's name on the brochures.
4 financing the mail shot.
5 a special advertising campaign by Excel in the Chicago area.

71

2   Listen again to the negotiations and note how the following things are done.

1   Finishing off point 1 of the agenda: *OK, I... point 1.*

2   Introducing point 2 of the agenda: *Let's ....point 2 then.*

3   Delaying a decision: *OK, OK. We'll .... and let you know.*

4   Making a proposal: *Why ...., two thirds-one third?*

5   Agreeing to a proposal: *It's ....*

3   Now you are going to continue the meeting. Look back to the agenda on page 70. You'll see that point 3 is *Technical back-up and sales training.* Be ready to compromise in order to reach agreement on this point.

Student B   Go to page 136.
Student A   You are Harold Goodman.

> You will invite two Bold Elextro sales engineers on a one week course to teach them about Excel products. The cost to Bold Elextro will be $500 per person.
>
> You will send Bold Elextro a copy of the magazine produced by the Excel R&D department. This gives details of new developments and products and comes out every three months.
>
> You will send technical manuals of all Excel products.

11.3   What's missing?

Work in pairs.

Student B   You go to page 136.
Student A   Ask your partner for the information to complete this contract.

> The Principal, Syncro Development Ltd, will supply the Agent [.................] with up to $70,000 worth of goods during each trading period of [.................]. The Principal will pay 10% commission on all goods sold. Commission will be paid annually in [.................]. The Agent will be the sole representative of the Principal in the states of [.................]. All insurance will be paid by the Principal, who will also bear [.................] of the advertising and promotion costs.

THE MILLION DOLLAR GAME

AN EIGHT-YEAR OLD BOY caused $1,000,000 worth of damage when the aeroplane he was travelling on called at Shannon Airport in Ireland for duty-free shopping and immigration formalities. The boy and his father were returning to New York on a Northwest Orient Airlines flight from Prestwick in Scotland, after a short European holiday.

Shocked airport officials told reporters that the father had left his son near the boarding gate while he went off to the duty-free shop. The boy found the controls of the airbridge and started playing with them. Before the airport staff could stop him, he had succeeded in moving the airbridge and had caused substantial damage to the front passenger door of the Boeing 747 Jumbo jet.

Technicians tried to repair the door, but had to call for help from the United States. Meanwhile the 400 passengers spent the night in a hotel near the airport, as the plane was unable to fly.

A spokesperson for Northwest Orient estimated that the final cost of repairs could be as high as $1,000,000. Already negotiations are under way to decide who will pay the bill.

Aer Lingus operate and maintain the airbridge, but it is owned by the Irish Airports Authority. So who pays? One person who isn't worrying at all is a little boy in New York, safe at home, playing with his toy aeroplanes!

11.4 When it all goes wrong

1 Who pays when things go wrong? Read this newspaper article and decide who should pay for the damage.

2 Answer the questions about the article.

1 Where was the boy travelling from and to?
2 Why did the plane land at Shannon?
3 What did the boy do while his father was away?
4 What happened to the 400 passengers?
5 Who repaired the damage?
6 Which three organizations are now discussing responsibility for the accident?
7 What's happened to the boy?

3 Find words in paragraphs 1-2 which mean:

1 entry into a foreign country   2 journalists   3 serious

Find words in paragraphs 3-5 which mean:

4 representative   5 formal discussions   6 keep in working order

11.5 On the spot – a fax from Lyon

1 Study this fax. What is it asking George Rosario to do?

```
Attention George Rosario
Please send a.s.a.p. full print-out of distributors/
agents for U.S. and Canada.  Also your report on
agents.  Have you had problems from customers using
your version of videophone system (EVP223/4)?
        Thanks Thierry
```

73

Over to you **2**   Write a fax message to Thierry Rombaud.

- Acknowledge his request.
- Promise to fax the information about the distributors as soon as possible.
- Promise to send your report on agents within one week.
- Promise to check with your agents to find out if they have had any problems with the videophone system.

Language focus – the Future Simple

1   One of the most important uses of the Future Simple *(will do)* is when we **promise** to do something. Look at the contract in 11.3. **Will** is used to show that both sides are agreeing and promising to do certain things in the future.

Put **will** into this dialogue in all the right places.

A: Can you send me the goods as soon as possible?

B: Yes. We .... deliver them tomorrow morning. We .... have a lot of

customers in your area. I .... send the invoice to your Accounts

Department at the same time. Do you know that we .... offer a guarantee

on all our products. Are you interested?

A: Yes. But can I see it first?

B: Of course. I .... put one in the post to you. We .... find that most of our

customers .... choose to take out a guarantee.

A: Do you have an agent in our area?

B: Yes. Friedlander's .... represent us. I .... tell Mr Banks, Friedlander's Sales

Manager, that you are one of our new customers. He .... contact you in a

week or so.

A: Thank you. I .... call you next month with another order.

B: Thank you. Goodbye.

2   **Predictions** are guesses about the future. We use **will** when we are talking about what we think will happen in the future.

*I think it **will** rain tomorrow.*
*We predict prices **will** rise a lot in the next six months.*
*We expect that the economy **will** continue to grow slowly in the coming year.*

Now work in small groups. What do *you* think will happen in the next six months to:

- the rate of inflation?
- the value of your currency against the US dollar?
- the price of oil?
- your country's economy?
- unemployment in your country?
- the cost of electronic products?

Use these adverbs to show whether you predict a small change or a big change.

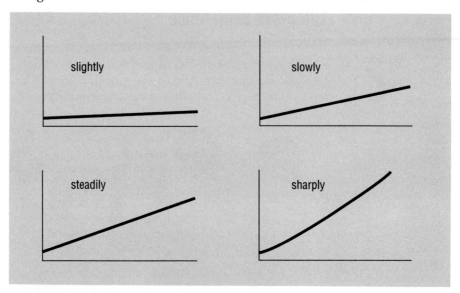

3 If someone presents you with a problem or an idea, you often react by saying what you'll do, e.g.

A: *I can't understand this telex from Spain.*
B: *I'll translate it for you.*

How would you react in these situations?

1 A: *I haven't got time to book the flight.*
B: ....

2 A: *We need three copies of the report immediately.*
B: ....

3 A: *I think it would be a good idea to hold the conference in Spain this year.*
B: ....

4 A: *This manual is so complicated. I don't understand a word of it.*
B: ....

NOTE See Unit 13 for information on the First Conditional (**will** in **if** sentences).

75

UNIT 12 *Excel in China*

In this unit you will:

- attend a press conference.
- arrange a one day sales conference.
- read about the problem of industrial pollution.
- discuss a staffing problem.

12.1 The press conference

1 Excel has big plans for the future. Suzie Taylor, Public Relations Director for Excel Europe, has called a press conference at the Lyon Head Office to tell the business world about a new development.

Listen to Suzie Taylor and write down what is going to happen at the press conference this morning. Some of the information is already on the timetable.

TIME	EVENT
9.30	....
....	The Chinese project
....	....
....	....

76

2   Here is part of the press release which Excel gives out to the journalists at
the press conference. Answer these questions about it.

1   What is the result of the Chinese trade delegation's visit to EC countries?
2   What is the value of the new contract?
3   What equipment will be supplied?
4   Who are the members of the consortium?

THE CHINESE CONNECTION

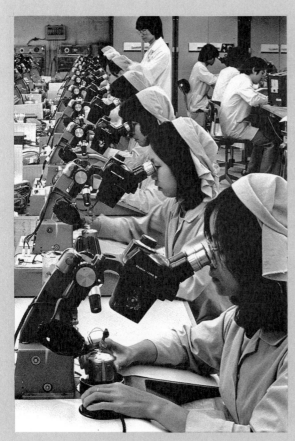

The People's Republic of China is one of the most important markets in the world for Western businesses. At Excel, we are playing our part in developing the Chinese economy. Recently, a trade delegation from Beijing visited the capitals of EC countries. The result is an important contract for a consortium of three European companies, led by Excel.

The consortium has secured a contract worth over $2 billion to supply advanced communication equipment over the next three years. The equipment is being bought by the Chinese media and communications industries.

Excel's partners in the consortium are BAS (British American Services), who manufacture a range of telecommunications equipment, including satellite systems, and Carter-Perry, the international financing company.

3   Look again at some of the longer words in the press release. Underline the
stressed syllable.

1   contract
2   equipment
3   advanced
4   important
5   consortium

6   financing
7   European
8   developing
9   capitals

4   Bill Timms, a reporter for an international news agency, wrote a short article after his visit to the Excel offices.

Fill in the missing words.

$2 bn CONTRACT FOR EURO CONSORTIUM IN CHINA

A huge .... worth $2 billion was announced by Mr Roberto Presutti yesterday at an Excel press

....

A .... of three important European .... will supply communication .... to

China over the next three ....

The contract follows a recent visit to European .... by a Chinese .... delegation. The

equipment is for the Chinese media and communications ....

Over to you   **5**   Your department is organizing a one day sales conference for all the sales managers in your company. You are responsible for planning the conference and for welcoming the guests.

1   Work in groups. Look at the list of talks and put them in a sensible order. You want to start at 10.00 am, lunch at 1.00, and finish at about 4.00 pm.

---

45 min	General discussion
90 min	Progress reports by Sales Managers
50 min	Presentation of new product range by Technical Development Team
90 min	Workshop : improving sales techniques – discussion in small groups, followed by full group discussion
30 min	European Sales Director – The Way Ahead
30 min	Financial Controller – Keeping Accurate Statistics
10 min	Introduction
60 min	Lunch
15 min	Coffee

---

2   Welcome your colleagues. Tell them what they are going to do during the conference.

Here are some phrases from Suzie Taylor's presentation which will help you.
Could I have your attention, please?
First of all, ...
I'd like to thank everybody for coming here today.
I want to tell you what's going to happen.
Please ask if you need more information.

12.2   Suzie Taylor interviewed

Bill Timms is interviewing Suzie Taylor about another project of Excel's, this time in Indonesia. Bill's research has produced the notes below. Now he wants to check the facts in an interview with Suzie.

Work in pairs.

Student B You are Suzie Taylor. Go to page 137 for your information.
Student A You are Bill Timms. Check that your information is correct and complete.

Contract for Excel to supply Indonesian government with EP12X electronic communication system. Government minister responsible: Mr Suharna, Minister for Armed Forces.

Value of contract: $½ billion

System to be used by Indonesian army to link active army units.

Special security system means that no one outside can listen into conversations.

System in operation next year.

System tested in Middle East and U.S.

12.3 Industry and ecology

1 Before you read this article about an industrial accident, discuss these questions with a partner:

1 What are the worst kinds of pollution in your country?
2 Should we manufacture chemicals which can kill people or pollute the environment?

2 Now read the article and answer the questions which follow on page 80.

DISASTER ON THE RHINE

A fire at a chemical plant in Basel, Switzerland, led to one of the worst ecological disasters of the last ten years.

Poisonous chemicals, including deadly mercury compounds, were released into the River Rhine following a warehouse fire at the huge Sandoz complex, just north of the city of Basel. The water near the factory turned pink, and scientists soon realized that a major ecological disaster had occurred. Within days, thousands of fish were found dead on the shores of the Rhine as the chemicals flowed slowly downstream through West Germany.

Analysis of the water showed that there was danger to human life as well as to fish and plants. Towns and villages near the Rhine had their drinking water delivered by tanker for over a week.

Further down the Rhine, the Dutch authorities could do nothing to stop the chemicals reaching their waters. They hoped that there would be no long-term damage to fish in the North Sea itself, but no one was sure what the effect would be.

Meanwhile, Sandoz conducted a full inquiry into the accident. At a press conference, there were angry scenes when protesters threw poisoned Rhine water at representatives of the Swiss pharmaceutical company.

Dead fish being collected by fishermen

1 Why did the chemicals flow into the River Rhine?
2 What were the effects on fish in the river?
3 What happened to the drinking water of towns and villages near the river?
4 What did the Dutch authorities do?
5 What did Sandoz do?
6 What did the protesters do?

3 Look at the second paragraph of the article. Find words which mean:

1 very big ....

2 happened ....

3 catastrophe ....

4 river banks ....

5 towards the sea ....

Look at the last two paragraphs. Find words which mean:

6 investigation ....

7 people with the power to make decisions ....

8 certain ....

9 permanent ....

12.4 On the spot

You are chairing a meeting of the Finance Committee of your company. Discuss with a partner the best way to do the following things in English:

1 start the meeting.
2 check that everybody has a copy of the agenda.
3 explain the reason for the meeting (*to agree expenditure for the next year*).
4 ask the members of the committee for their ideas.
5 ask a speaker to finish off what they have to say.
6 deal with an interruption by a speaker who wants to talk about production problems.
7 promise to discuss a particular project (*the Excel FR2*) at the next meeting.
8 tell the committee members the date of the next meeting.
9 close the meeting.

12.5 Off to China

1 Excel, BAS and Carter-Perry are the members of the Chinese consortium. They have to appoint a Project Coordinator to lead the consortium in China. On the next page is some information about the consortium's project. Study it.

CONSORTIUM'S ACTIVITIES IN CHINA

Telecommunications

Phase 1: Review of existing systems, hardware, work volume (liaison with Chinese government).
Phase 2: Recommendations for new equipment and systems.
Phase 3: Trials of new systems in limited geographical area.
Phase 4: Implementation of new system on nationwide basis.
Phase 5: Troubleshooting - dealing with any problems with the system.
Training Chinese nationals to operate and maintain the system.

Timescale - 3 years

---

2 Your task is to choose a Project Coordinator. He or she will be in charge of five consortium employees and 20 locally recruited employees. The contract will be for a minimum of two years.

Write down your ideas under these headings.

Age:
Sex:
Marital status:
Education:
Experience:
Knowledge of languages:

3 Now listen to the consortium's discussion of the same subject. Note down their opinions and compare them with those of your group.

Language focus – Going to

1 We use **going to** to talk about our **plans** and **intentions** for the future. As you saw in the last unit, we use **will** when we make promises or predictions about the future.

Look at these exchanges. Choose the best answer.

1 A: When is your appointment with BCM?
   B: I'm going to see them on Wednesday.
   B: I'll see them on Wednesday.
2 A: Could I see your report on Japanese imports?
   B: Of course. I'm going to send you a copy today.
   B: Of course. I'll send you a copy today.
3 A: Can we discuss this further?
   B: Yes, I am going to phone you tomorrow.
   B: Yes, I'll phone you tomorrow.

81

4 A: The competition from Korea is very strong.
   B: Yes, what are we going to do about it?
   B: Yes, what will we do about it?
5 A: What about plans for next year?
   B: We're going to open a new factory in Spain.
   B: We will open a new factory in Spain.

2 Now write answers to these questions. You are Roberto. Use **going to**
or **will.**

A: Roberto, have you any plans for this afternoon?

B: ....

A: I see. That report on the Matthews account is very urgent. When can you
give it to me?

B: ....

A: That's fine. By the way, which department is Charles Temple going to
work for?

B: ....

A: Mmm. Can you ask him to come and see me as soon as possible?

B: ....

3 Sometimes information we have now means that we can be quite sure what
will happen in the future. In this situation we often use **going to,** e.g. *Paul is*
going to retire *next year. He's 64, you know.*

Write sentences about the future with **going to**, using the information you
have about the present.

1 There is a big 'For Sale' sign outside the factory.

company/close ....

a lot of people/lose jobs ....

2 The strike started yesterday.

company/lose a lot of money..

deliveries/be late ....

3 The company has signed a $2.5 billion contract.

company/make big profit this year ....

company/take on more staff ....

UNIT 13   *Holidays for a lifetime*

In this unit you will:

- talk about and listen to a discussion on salesmanship.
- read about and discuss timeshare holiday schemes.
- choose the Salesperson of the Year.
- make social contacts.

13.1   The ideal salesperson

1   Before you listen to a discussion about the ideal salesperson, decide with a partner which of these qualities are most important in a salesperson: *persuasive, friendly, hardworking, charismatic, physically attractive, independent, enthusiastic.*

 2   Harold Goodman is over in Lyon from Boston for a sales strategy meeting. At the meeting there is a discussion about what makes an ideal salesperson. Note down what Harold and his colleagues say on this subject.

3   Here are some ideas on improving the motivation of a sales team.

- organize a competition
- provide the sales team with a uniform
- hold regular sales conferences
- increase the rate of commission
- send the sales team on a training course
- increase salaries
- provide the sales team with larger company cars
- pay a special bonus for salespeople who think up new ideas

Which do *you* think are the best ideas? Put them in order of importance (1 to 8). Can you think of any other ideas.

 4   In the second part of their meeting, Harold Goodman and his colleagues discuss how to improve the motivation of the Excel sales team. Listen and note which of the ideas above are mentioned at the meeting.

5   Now listen again to both parts of the meeting and complete these sentences.

The ideal salesperson

1 *Yes, but if they don't have the technical knowledge,* ....

2 *And if they don't have the personality,* ....

3 *If you get depressed and give up in that situation,* ....

Motivation is the key

4 *If we pay the salesforce more money,* ....

5 .... *unless they actually work harder.*

6 *If we make them all feel part of Excel,* ....

13.2 **The competition**

1   After much discussion, it was agreed to offer the prize of a timeshare holiday apartment to the top salesperson. Read the article on the next page and explain what a timeshare is.

TIMESHARE
HOLIDAYS FOR A LIFETIME

Timesharing is the new way to plan and enjoy your holidays - this year, next year and on into the future. This is how the scheme works.

Just choose your favourite holiday destination. You're sure to find a number of timeshare schemes operating there. Most timeshares are private flats, apartments, cottages or villas. You don't buy the property or rent it. You buy the right to use it for a certain period of time each year - for ever!

But what happens when, after five years, you're tired of staying in the same apartment in the Algarve in Portugal and want to go somewhere else? Simple. You join a timeshare exchange club which will arrange, for a small fee, to find someone to stay in your apartment while you go off for two weeks to Austria, Andorra or Alaska!

One word of warning, however. Don't believe the salesman when he tells you what a good investment timeshares are. It isn't always easy to find someone who wants to spend two weeks in November on the Costa del Sol for the rest of their life!

The return on your investment is not financial. It's the opportunity you have to visit places all over the world and stay in high-quality private accommodation wherever you go.

2 Are these statements about timesharing **true** or **false**?

1 Under a timeshare agreement you don't buy the apartment or villa.
2 A timeshare exchange club will sell your timeshare to someone else.
3 It costs nothing to belong to a timeshare exchange club.
4 Investing in a timeshare is a good way to make money in the future.

● Would *you* be interested in investing in a timeshare?

3 Find the pairs of words which mean the same?

1 plan *(noun)*   **A** flat
2 opportunity   **B** operate
3 salesman   **C** chance
4 work *(verb)*   **D** scheme
5 apartment   **E** select
6 choose *(verb)*   **F** representative

85

Over to you **4** You are members of the committee which has to decide who wins the prize for Salesperson of the Year. Work in groups and decide who *you* think should be Salesperson of the Year.

Here are some phrases which you will find useful during the discussion:

On balance, I think ... should get the prize, because ...
I think we should choose ... because ...
As far as I'm concerned, ...
That may be true, but ...
You have a point there, but ...
If you look at the figures for ... , you'll see that ...

TOM LUNDGREN - has worked for Excel in Scandinavia for ten years. Responsible for selling a videophone system to the Swedish government.
JANE FORTUNA - Excel, Boston. Took over as USA Sales Coordinator for radio-controlled systems two years ago.
JEAN-OLIVIER DRAI - Head Office, Lyon. Sells communications software packages to industrial customers in France.
ENRICO BATTISTINI - technical salesman in Middle East area. An expert on selling and installing information networking systems.

	Total No. of customers	Total value of sales ($000)	Sales targets ($000)	No. of products sold	%ge of new customers
TL	8	480	410	12	70%
JF	17	450	350	10	34%
JOD	15	440	400	5	45%
EB	2	560	525	1	50%

13.3 The timeshare brochure

1 Klaus Jensen has a timeshare apartment in Megeve, a skiing resort in the French Alps. This year he wants a more exotic holiday and so he has joined a timeshare exchange club. Look at five of the entries in the brochure. In groups or pairs, discuss what Klaus will be able to see and do at each holiday location.

FOREST HILLS ESTATE, SCOTLAND

The 22 acres of magnificent parkland of the Moor Hills Estate surround these uniquely-designed apartments. Built next to the Moor Hills Hotel and on the edge of sparkling Loch Ard, the apartments all command a superb view over mountain, lake and moorland. Edinburgh and Glasgow are just one hour's drive away but Loch Lomond and Stirling Castle are even closer. There is excellent trout fishing on the Loch.

FULL MOON CLUB, MONTEGO BAY, JAMAICA

A rich history, spectacular scenery, sandy beaches and a superb climate have made Jamaica a world famous holiday island. The Full Moon Club is one of the world's finest resorts with luxurious accommodation, a beautiful private beach, and an extensive list of amenities. At local marinas, you can hire boats for fishing or sailing. The colourful local markets are well worth a visit.

NOBB HILL HOTEL, SAN FRANCISCO, CALIFORNIA, USA

Built on one of San Francisco's 40 hills, Nobb Hill Hotel lays at your feet all the excitement and elegance of this famous city: Fisherman's Wharf, the Golden Gate Bridge and a host of museums and galleries. By night, San Francisco really comes to life and you can watch the city glittering below you from one of the famous hotels. At the day's end, Nobb Hill Hotel surrounds you with elegance and luxury.

PHEELAN HOUSE, LONDON, ENGLAND

Situated in the Royal Borough of Kensington and Chelsea, Pheelan House is close to all that London has to offer. Famous stores such as Harrods, theatres and museums are all to hand as are the beautiful Kensington Gardens and Hyde Park. The elegant apartments are ideal for family or business entertaining and there is a garden which residents can use. Trains, taxis and buses are all nearby.

SORRENTO, ITALY

In the south of Italy, 40 km from Naples is the family resort of Sorrento. The complex is in a very quiet location overlooking the blue Tyrrhenian Sea. Within the complex are a supermarket

and a self-service restaurant serving local style meals. A mini-club for children offers a range of activities.

2   Discuss which of the five holiday destinations will be best for these people.

Karen Hashman, 29, from Los Angeles, Commercial Director. Enjoys quiet, luxurious holidays in exotic locations.

Harry Cooke, 37, from Manchester, Electronics Engineer for Hambrown Ltd., with his wife and young family (James, 4 and Alison, $2\frac{1}{2}$. Likes active, sporty holidays. Needs lively centre with lots of entertainment for children.

Hans Weidemann, 58, from Dusseldorf, Project Manager, UMAG, with his wife and children (aged 19 and 17). Likes travelling to new places. Interested in different cultures, good food.

Claudia Bernetti, 25, fashion designer from Milan, and her boyfriend, Paolo Beltramo, a photographer. They want to go to exciting holiday destinations, with plenty of sun and sand and nightlife, but want to keep away from tourists on package holidays.

13.4   On the spot

1   You are on a timeshare exchange holiday in Florida. What would you say in these situations to an American neighbour?

You want to:
1 change some traveller's cheques.
2 borrow some salt.
3 invite your neighbours in for a drink.
4 ask about places of interest nearby.
5 ask for recommendations about local restaurants.
6 call the doctor.

2   Now work in pairs. You are neighbours in a timeshare villa resort.

Student A

Introduce yourself.
Ask your neighbour if s/he is having a good time.
Ask about his/her family.
Invite him/her to a barbeque.
Make arrangements about the time and place.

Student B

Be ready to answer Student A's questions.
Ask about his/her family and where s/he comes from.
Accept Student A's invitation. Offer to bring something.

Language focus – The First Conditional

1 Our plans for the future are never certain. Sometimes one event in the future depends on another, so we use the **First Conditional** construction.

*If we **have** enough money, we **will invest** in a timeshare.*
*If we **join** a timeshare exchange club, we **will be able to visit** lots of interesting places.*
*If we **buy** a timeshare, we **will** always **have** somewhere to go on holiday.*

Don't forget the most important rule about the **First Conditional:** the verb after **if** is always in the **Present Tense**.

2 Put the word **will** in all the right places in this paragraph.

> If we .... find a way to motivate all the sales force, we .... have a much
>
> better year next year. Maybe, motivation .... increase if we .... pay higher
>
> salaries. The important thing is to make people feel part of Excel. If we ....
>
> hold a conference for them in the best hotel in town, they .... see that we
>
> really care about them.

3 **Unless** means **if not**, e.g. **Unless** *we* **do** *something quickly, sales* **will** *start to fall.*

Put **if** or **unless** into these sentences.

1 We'll improve the sales team's motivation .... we pay them more money.

2 We won't improve the sales team's motivation .... we pay them more money.

3 I think I'll close the meeting now .... anyone has any more ideas.

4 .... you have any more ideas, please send them to me by the end of the week.

5 I'll send out a memo to the sales staff .... anyone else would prefer to do it.

6 I think we should write an article about the winner in our in-house journal, ... he or she agrees.

UNIT 14   *Next point on the agenda*

In this unit you will:

- listen in on a phone call and a meeting.
- read and discuss a consultant's report.
- decide on company policy and write a short report on it.
- read about new telecommunications technology.

14.1 Agenda for the meeting

Here is the provisional agenda for a meeting at Excel Europe next week. Listen to a telephone conversation between Henrik Thorsen and Jean Gaudrie about that meeting. Fill in the missing information and change the agenda as necessary.

Agenda for the .... Committee to be held in

.... on ....

1. Minutes of the last meeting.
2. Matters arising.
3. Report on Indonesian project.
4. Financial targets for 3 year plan.
5. Date of next meeting.
6. A.O.B.

Jean Gaudrie
Chairman

14.2 Consultant's report

1   Excel bought Digital Communications, a software engineering company, three years ago. The company has not performed well. The R&D Department has not come up with any new products and the existing product range is now becoming obsolescent. Sales have fallen each year since the takeover. The situation has been made worse by the availability of new software engineering systems from the Far East.

Excel has asked McKay Whitney, a firm of management consultants, to investigate the problem and produce a report on Digital Communications. At the Planning Committee meeting, Excel executives have to discuss the report and decide what action to take.

Read the final part of the report. What are the major recommendations?

MCKAY WHITNEY

INTERNATIONAL MANAGEMENT CONSULTANTS

---

page 14

which the Client is advised to introduce as soon as can be arranged, if any improvements are to be made in the near future in the company's performance.

SUMMARY

The main findings of this Report may be summarized as follows:

1. DC's most serious problem is its product range. With the existing product range, we cannot see a secure future for the company.
2. We have interviewed all management staff. There are a lot of ideas for new products/activities. We believe the expertise is there to develop successful new products.
3. DC top management is not strong. Liaison between DC executives and Excel executives is not good. This leads to uncertainty at DC and a lack of long-term planning.

RECOMMENDATIONS

1. A complete review of the existing product range.
2. A market survey to establish the need for new products in Europe and the US.
3. A market survey to establish if the existing product range can be sold effectively in developing countries (Africa, Latin America).
4. A three-year investment programme in R&D, including training of key technical personnel, recruiting new technical experts. Aim: to develop new products.
5. Appointment of a 'troubleshooter', a senior Excel manager, who will make sure that DC is well managed and has good liaison with the parent company.

Peter Kornfeld

Peter Kornfeld
Senior Consultant

---

2   Here is some vocabulary from the summary of McKay Whitney's report. Find the correct definitions.

1 *findings*   means   a) answers.
                        b) questions.
                        c) conclusions.
2 *secure*   means   a) safe.
                        b) helpful.
                        c) possible.
3 *expertise* means   a) technology.
                        b) know-how.
                        c) experience.
4 *liaison*   means   a) friendship.
                        b) regular contact.
                        c) agreement.

91

3 Now look again at McKay Whitney's recommendations. Say if these statements are **true** or **false**.

McKay Whitney thinks that Excel should:
1 develop new products.
2 advertise on TV.
3 appoint a troubleshooter.
4 employ more salespeople.
5 try to sell existing products.
6 find new managers for the company.
7 survey the European/US market.
8 manufacture products in the developing countries.

Over to you **4** Now work in groups. Look again at the five recommendations. Should Excel accept or reject them? What would *you* do in this situation?

14.3 At the meeting

1 Listen to part of the Planning Committee meeting. The members of the committee are discussing point 5 of McKay Whitney's recommendations.

There are **two** arguments for and **two** arguments against the appointment of a troubleshooter. What are they?

2 Listen again to the meeting and complete these phrasal verbs?

1 Can we **move** .... to point 5 now?

2 ... the most important recommendation McKay Whitney have **come** ....

3 ... we'd be sure that they'd **keep** .... the budgets ...

4 ... actually followed the policy we **laid** ....

5 I think we should **go** .... and appoint this troubleshooter as soon as possible.

6 ... I'm sure their directors could **turn** the company ....

14.4 What should Digital Communications do?

1 Imagine you are the troubleshooter. You have to decide what to do with Digital Communications. Work in groups and discuss what to do in each situation. Follow the maze and find out what happens. Keep a note of your decisions and your route through the maze.

1	SALES OF DC SYSTEMS FALLING		
	● Appoint new management team.	▸	GOTO 3
	● Invest in new products.	▸	GOTO 7
	● Take on new salespeople.	▸	GOTO 4
2	DC A1 SYSTEM A GREAT SUCCESS		
	● Open bottle of champagne to celebrate.	▸	END
3	NEW MANAGEMENT TEAM UNSUCCESSFUL AFTER TWELVE MONTHS		
	● Fire new managers.	▸	GOTO 1
	● Give them another six months.	▸	GOTO 6
4	SALES TEAM INCREASE TURNOVER BY ONLY 6%		
	● Change investment to R & D.	▸	GOTO 7
	● Do nothing.	▸	GOTO 1
5	EXCEL SAYS 'NO MORE MONEY'		
	● Take no immediate action.	▸	GOTO10
	● Ask consultant's advice.	▸	GOTO 9
6	END OF YEAR PROFITS LOW		
	● Raise prices.	▸	GOTO 1
	● Cut back development programme.	▸	GOTO 8
7	DEVELOPMENT COSTS INCREASING		
	● Continue to invest in research and development.	▸	GOTO 6
	● Cut back development programme.	▸	GOTO 8
8	SHARE PRICE FALLING		
	● Ask shareholders (Excel) for more money.	▸	GOTO 5
	● Ask bank for help.	▸	GOTO 9
9	R&D DEVELOP EXCITING NEW PRODUCT		
	● Develop product with consortium.	▸	GOTO 2
	● Ask shareholders (Excel) for development money.	▸	GOTO 5
10	THE END OF THE ROAD		
	● Excel sells DC : DC closes down.	▸	END

2 Write a paragraph saying what happened when you followed the maze?
Start like this: *Sales of DC systems were falling, so we decided to appoint a new
management team. Then ...*

Here are some phrases you can use:

After that, we decided to ...   *We agreed to ...*
Then we tried ...   *In the end, ...*

3 Look at the definitions and provide the missing words.

   1 total value of sales: *t*.................
   2 group of companies: *c*.................
   3 owners of public company: *s*.................
   4 scientific study: *r*.................
   5 money spent for future profit: *i*.................

14.5 The Telecom Fair

1   Read this article about new developments in the telecommunications field and answer the questions which follow.

• DIGITAL • PHONE • REVOLUTION •

When telephoning friends in Australia, would you like to see pictures of them at the same time? When calling a garage about a broken car, would you like to look at the diagrams in a parts catalogue? When discussing financial figures, would you like to have them transferred into your own desk-top computer?

All this can be done now – by big businesses with the money and expertise required. But in a few years ordinary people should be able to do the same.

This became clear at the Telecom Fair, a trade exhibition and conference for the world's telecommunications community in Geneva earlier this month.

There are facsimile machines able to transmit a document in six seconds (compared with the present 60 seconds) and one that can transmit in colour. There are picture phones which send and display a series of still photographs of the people talking on the line. And there are drawing pads which allow your doodles to appear on another pad at the receiving end.

The technology for integrating communication services over a digital network is available now. But the telecommunications world has not yet defined all the standards necessary for a truly global network to emerge. This could take up to ten years.

In the future, terminals will look very different from normal telephone handsets. They will have video screens, typewriter keyboards, drawing pads or printing devices.

It is possible to have an intelligent terminal which could read a credit card, send data automatically to the computer centre, and then have the person say a few words into the telephone for the computer to recognize the voice pattern before authorization. It should work well unless you have a heavy cold!

1 Who was the Telecom Fair for?
2 How will telephone terminals look in the future?
3 Why will it take up to ten years for a global network to emerge?
4 What are   a) facsimile machines?
                  b) picture phones?
                  c) drawing pads?
5 What can an intelligent terminal do?

2   Join the words to make phrases.

1	video	A	exhibition
2	credit	B	computers
3	digital	C	screens
4	typewriter	D	card
5	desk-top	E	network
6	trade	F	patterns
7	voice	G	keyboards

14.6 On the spot

What *would* you do in these situations? What *should* you do in these situations? There may be a difference!

1 You find a gold watch in your hotel bedroom on the day of your arrival.
2 At Christmas a client gives you a case of fine wine. You know that this gift is taxable in your country.
3 You're offered the job of opening a representative's office in China. You will have to spend the next two years there, with only six weeks' leave a year. You can't take your husband/wife with you.
4 By chance, you see your personal file. Some of the information is not correct and could mean that your chances for promotion are not so good.
5 One of your staff is having problems with his/her marriage. Your boss thinks your colleague's work is not as good as usual and asks you for a confidential report.
6 You are responsible for ordering expensive technical equipment. One supplier offers you a free holiday for yourself and a friend, if you place an order with him.
7 It's nine pm and you still haven't finished writing a report which is already one day late.
8 You are entertaining a business visitor for the evening. He says he would like to go to the ballet. You don't like the ballet at all.
9 You are invited to a colleague's farewell party. You have tickets for the theatre on the same evening.
10 You hit a car late at night in a car park and cause a small amount of damage. There is no one around.

Language focus – Would and Should

1 We can use **would** and **should** when we give our opinions or make recommendations about something.

Use **should** to give your opinion about other people.
*You **should** appoint a new Managing Director.*
*We think you **should** develop new products.*
*You **should** train your staff better.*

Use **would** to imagine yourself in a situation.
*I **would** try to improve sales of existing products.*
*I think I **would** find a new Managing Director.*
*We **would** ask a management consultant for advice.*

2   Put **would** or **should** in each gap in the following paragraph.

In your position, I .... try to develop new products. You .... invest in new equipment to reduce your production costs and .... tell your workers why you are doing this. I .... not employ more sales staff this year, but .... plan to increase the sales staff by 25% next year. You .... not give any interviews to the press about your plans. I .... tell them absolutely nothing.

3   The Second Conditional

We also use **would** with the second conditional. Look at these examples and note how to make this construction.

*If he **came** through that door now, I **would tell** him what I think of his report. They **would** certainly **be** here if they **weren't** so busy.*

The speaker in both these sentences is imagining a situation which is **possible** but **unlikely.**

4   What would you do in these unlikely situations?

Example: A fire starts in your office.

If a fire started in my office, I would press the fire alarm.

1   An order from Greenland arrives on your desk.
2   You can't turn the computer system off.
3   Your boss suggests a meeting on Sunday afternoon.
4   You miss your flight to the United States.
5   A visitor arrives for an appointment with you two hours early.
6   The lift you're travelling in stops between floors.

15.1   Making arrangements

1   You attended the Geneva Telecommunications Exhibition last month and made several useful contacts. You receive this letter at your office in Excel's headquarters in Lyon.

1 Who is the letter from?
2 What is the writer interested in?
3 Why has he written the letter?

GOC   **GRYFON OIL**
CORPORATION
123-125 Charles Street
Bombay
INDIA

30 October 19...

Dear ....

At our meeting at the Geneva
Telecommunications Exhibition last month I
expressed our possible interest in your range
of Radio Data Transmission Systems (RDTS).

I shall be in France for the week beginning 2
December and should like to take the
opportunity to visit you to discuss our
requirements.

I look forward to hearing from you.

Yours sincerely

Ranjit Singh

Ranjit Singh

Administrative Director

---

2   This is your reply. Complete the letter using one word in each gap.

Dear Mr Singh

Thank you for your letter of 30 .... We are pleased to hear of your

.... in our Radio Data Transmission Systems, and shall be delighted to

.... you to our Lyon .... in early December.

Perhaps you would .... me know which day would be .... for

you. If you have time, we would .... to include a tour of the production

unit, followed by lunch with myself and our Production Director.

I look .... to hearing from you again shortly.

Yours ....

15.2   A fax from Mr Singh

```
Thank you for your letter concerning my proposed visit.  I am
able to see you on Tuesday 3 December at 8.30 am.  Please
confirm asap.
Regards
Ranjit Singh
```

Ranjit Singh

Send a reply by fax to Mr Singh.

- Thank him for his fax.
- Confirm the date.
- Offer to reserve a hotel room.
- Offer to meet him at the airport.
- Ask him to confirm his flight number and arrival time.

15.3   Replying to a memo

1   After sending Mr Singh the fax, you receive the memo on the next page.

1 When is the next planning meeting? Are you still able to attend?
2 What does Christine Louis remind committee members to do?

To: All members, Staff Training Committee
From: Christine Louis, Personnel Department
Date: 5 November
Subject: Staff Training Planning Meeting

The next planning meeting scheduled for Tuesday 26 November has to be postponed for one week. The new date is Tuesday December 3 at 8.30 in the Training Centre.

   I hope that all members will still be able to attend. Could I also remind you that your breakdown of future training needs for your department should reach me by 19 November?

Thank you.

2   The new date for the meeting is the same as the date you have confirmed for your meeting with Mr Singh. You decide that the meeting with Mr Singh is more important. Complete the memo to Christine Louis explaining your reason for not attending. Give the information she requests. Remember this is a formal memo.

To: Christine Louis, Personnel Department

From: ....

Date: ....

Subject: Staff Training ....

I regret that .... the meeting on 3 December as

.... on that day to discuss ....

Please find .... a breakdown of .... ,

as ....

15.4 An invitation

Later on, you receive this note from a colleague. Write a note in reply to this invitation, explaining that you cannot come. This time your reply is less formal.

> We are having a buffet lunch for Liliane Menton,
>   Customer Support Services,
> on Tuesday 3 December to celebrate her promotion.
>   Can you come?

15.5 A second letter from India

After the visit by Mr Singh, you receive this letter from him.

**GRYFON OIL
CORPORATION**
123-125 Charles Street
Bombay
INDIA

                                10 December 19....

Dear ....

Thank you very much for a most useful and
constructive visit last week. I was most impressed
by everything I saw. I believe that, with a few
changes, your equipment will meet our requirements.

I shall be in touch with you again early next year,
when we expect to be able to place a firm order.

Your sincerely

Ranjit Singh

Ranjit Singh
Administrative Director

1 Is the equipment suitable?
2 Was the visit successful?
3 Why is Mr Singh going to write again in the new year?

15.6 Beginning and ending letters

1 The opening and closing sentences are in the wrong order here.

Match the columns. One of the pairs has been done for you.

1 Dear Sirs
With reference to our letter of 24 April
we must request that ...

A I'll phone next week to confirm
arrangements.
Kind regards
Eric

2 Dear Mr Aota
We were very sorry to receive your
letter about ...

B My thanks to you again for all your help
in this project.
With best wishes,
Yours sincerely
Raymond Jones

3 Dear Mr Hoffman
Further to your recent telephone enquiry,
we are pleased to enclose a copy of
our current ...

C I hope therefore that this will not happen
again.
Yours sincerely
Paul Goodman

4 Dear Anna
Just a note to let you know that I shall be in
Stockholm for three days and ...

D If we do not receive your written
acceptance by 30 May, we shall have to
reconsider our offer.
Yours faithfully
P. J. McKenzie

5 Dear Andrew
I understand from the Regional Sales
Manager that you have been late in
submitting your last three monthly reports
...

E If you require any further information,
please do not hesitate to contact us.
Yours sincerely
S. Puglia

6 Dear Liliane
Thank you very much for sending me
the information on ...

F In the meantime, please accept our sincere
apologies for any inconvenience this may
have caused.
Yours sincerely
Maria Caballero

2 Answer these questions.

1 Which of the letters are friendly?
2 Which ones are formal and which are informal?
3 What do you think is the reason for writing each letter?

3 Now choose one of the pairs and write the letter that fits between the
opening and closing sentences. Work in small groups for this task.

UNIT 16 *Executive stress*

In this unit you will:

● discuss and read about the problem of stress.
● take part in a discussion on absences from work.
● ask for and give permission to do something.

16.1 Stressful situations

1 Look at these pictures. Which situations do you find stressful? Give a rating of 0 to 10 for each situation. Discuss your reactions with your partner.

● In what other situations do you feel stress?

2 Before you read the article on stress, answer these questions.

1 How do you deal with the problem of stress?
2 Can you name three medical problems which are linked with stress?
3 How do you keep fit?

DANGER – BUSINESS PEOPLE AT WORK!

Stress is a perfectly natural part of living. Crossing a road, going to a party, driving a car, these are all stressful activities. We live in a fast-moving age, so we must learn how to relax properly. Here are some of the most common symptoms of stress: sleeping badly, poor appetite or overeating, drinking too much alcohol, difficulty in concentrating. Long-term stress is associated with high blood pressure, headaches and heart disease.

But how do you deal with these problems? The average business person often doesn't have time to sit down and work out the answers. But if you want to survive, you have to know how to cope with stress. So here's a handy guide to reducing the level of stress in your life.

First, take up a hobby, if possible an active outdoor activity. You won't worry about your problems when you are concentrating on a hobby that really interests you.

You must take plenty of exercise. This will keep you fit and should also help you to sleep better. Exercise, combined with a healthy diet, will also help to keep your weight at the right level.

At work, it's important to make lists of tasks that you need to complete during the day. Write down your thoughts and ideas on paper. Set realistic deadlines that you can be sure to achieve. It's essential to take proper breaks during the day, so that you don't become too tired - taking time out for yourself isn't selfish, it makes good sense. Learn to say 'no', even to your boss, if you think that colleagues are being unreasonable. And finally, don't forget that laughter is the best medicine.

Start this new action plan today and you'll find, within a surprisingly short time, that stress at work and at home is no longer the problem it was.

3 Complete the following sentences, using the information in the article.

1 One way to keep fit is to ....

2 High blood pressure and heart disease are ....

3 A good way to reduce stress at work is to ....

4 Taking up a new hobby is a good idea because ....

5 If you follow this new action plan, ...

16.2 Performance review

Charles Slater at Excel Europe has a problem with stress. He discusses the situation with Christine Louis of the Personnel Department at his annual performance review. Listen to the conversation and note down:

1 the problems he's been having at work.
2 Christine Louis's suggestions for dealing with stress.
3 his reactions to the suggestions.

16.3 Stress reducers

Look at this list of stress reducers. Discuss with a partner which of these ideas would be useful for you and why.

In your personal life	You	Your partner
take up yoga		
discuss your problems with a friend		
take more exercise		
start a new hobby		
At work	**You**	**Your partner**
learn to say 'no'		
concentrate on one thing at a time		
take time out for yourself		
set realistic deadlines		
write down your thoughts and ideas		

● What other ideas do you or your partner have on how to deal with the problem of stress?

16.4 A healthy workforce

1 One of the results of stress is illness. Henri Flechon, the Medical Officer at Excel Europe, is giving a talk to his colleagues based on recent statistics.

On the next page is the handout which Henri distributes to his audience. Listen and fill in information about the numbers of days lost at Excel.

Days lost

The audited figures for days lost in this country last year are shown below. Holiday entitlements are not included in these figures.

	National	EXCEL
Total no. of days lost	205.5 million	....
Average % of absences on any one day	2.61%	....

Causes of absence	National	EXCEL
long-term sickness/injury	24%	....
colds/influenza	18%	....
back problems	12%	....
eye strain/headaches	11%	....
nervous/psychiatric problems	4%	....
no reason	10%	....
accidents	2%	....
stomach disorders	10%	....
minor medical problems	9%	....

2 Listen again to Henri Flechon talking. How does he:

1 welcome his guests?
2 distribute the handout?
3 ask people to share handouts?
4 focus everyone's attention on a particular point?
5 give instructions to get into groups?

Over to you **3** Your task is to work in groups and analyze the information Henri has given you.

1 Note down the differences between the national and Excel illness rates.
2 Decide (as far as you can) what the reasons are for the differences. Use the information in *Trends in Excel* below.
3 Suggest some solutions.
4 Present your group's ideas to the other groups.

Use the phrases you noted in **2** to help you present your ideas effectively.

Trends in Excel

Introduction of VDU terminals in Excel offices
New air conditioning systems installed
Double shift system introduced at some Excel factories
Flu epidemic in Jan/Feb last year
Increased productivity agreement between management and staff representatives

16.6 Word work

1 Look at this list of words which appear in this unit. Underline the stressed syllable.

1	concentrate	4	realistic	7	exercise
2	deadlines	5	seminar	8	statistics
3	psychological	6	approximately	9	ideas

2 Look again at the list of words above. Put each of them in the correct place in this paragraph.

> We need to .... (1) on the problem of the number of days lost. At this
>
> .... (2) today I want to give you the latest .... (3).
>
> .... (4) 3,000 days were lost last year. The main problems were not
>
> physical, but .... (5). There are many.................. (6) about how to
>
> solve the problem, but not all of them are .... (7). Of course, general
>
> fitness is very important and we must make sure that our employees take lots
>
> of .... (8). If we can reduce the number of days lost, we will be more
>
> efficient and we will be better able to keep to production .... (9).

16.7 On the spot – asking for and giving permission

1 It is very important to have good relations with colleagues, customers and business partners. Sometimes you have a problem which will also make life difficult for other people. In these circumstances, you may have to ask permission for something very politely.

Listen to the cassette. Note down each request, the reason for it and whether permission is given or not.

	Request	Reason	Permission given?
1	....	....	....
2	....	....	....
3	....	....	....
4	....	....	....

Here are some more ways of making requests or asking for permission.

Would you mind if ...?
Do you think we/you/I could ...?
Would it be possible to ...?
Is it all right if I/we ...?

2 When we give reasons for the request, we often use: *I must ...., I have to ....*
or *I've got to ....*
Which of these phrases **wouldn't** you use in written English?

Now ask your partner if you can do these things. Before you start, think of
a good reason for your request. Your partner should say if that is OK
or not.

1 You want to leave a meeting before it's finished.
2 You want to fly to Barcelona two days later than planned.
3 You want to employ an extra secretary in your department.
4 You want to hold the meeting in English, not in French.
5 You want to arrange an evening meeting with your boss.

Language focus – Obligation and necessity

CBarsotti

"No, Hoskins, you're not going to do it just
because I'm telling you to do it. You're going to
do it because you believe in it."

1 We use **must**, **have to** and **need to** to show that something is necessary. We
also use phrases like *It's essential that ...* and *It's important that ...* .
We use **mustn't** to show that something is not allowed.
We use **don't/doesn't have to** and **don't/doesn't need to** to show that
something is not necessary.
We also use **needn't do** to say an action is not necessary.

Here are some examples.

1 *You **must** show your identity card when you enter the building, but you **don't have to** sign your name in the Visitors' Book.*
2 *It's **essential/important** to stay with the visiting party at all times.*
3 *You **mustn't** leave your Identity Card in the building.*
4 *At the end of the tour, we would like to offer you a cup of coffee, but of course you **needn't** stay if you don't have time.*

2 Now look at this paragraph. A guide is showing visitors around part of Excel's factory in Lyon. Put **must, mustn't, don't have to, doesn't have to, need to** or **needn't** in the gaps.

> Please follow me, ladies and gentlemen. I'm afraid you .... (1) smoke in the Data Processing Department - the computers don't like it! You .... (2) wear any special clothing - only these white hats, if you don't mind. Before we go in, I .... (3) remind you that you are not allowed to take any photographs. If you have a camera with you, you .... (4) leave it here at Reception. You .... (5) worry, they'll be quite safe. And don't forget, if you .... (6) rush off home after the tour, please join us for a drink in the Hospitality Lounge. Right, then, this way please.

Training abroad

In this unit you will:

● find out about a training course in the UK.
● discuss ideas about the content of a training course.
● listen to a lecture on cross-cultural communications.
● read an article about office life.
● discuss how to react in difficult situations.

17.1 Opportunities abroad

 1 Christine Louis is on a European tour of eight Excel companies and subsidiaries. She is interviewing young trainees and hoping to select one from each company to follow a six-month management training course in the UK. Listen to her talking to Giorgio Casini in Milan.

   1 Write down the following details about the course:
   a) the location.   c) the length of the course.
   b) the starting date.   d) the accommodation.
   2 What **three** reasons does Giorgio give for wanting to follow this programme?
   3 Giorgio had problems with the words **ambitious** and **overview**. Can you explain what they mean?

2 Listen again to the conversation between Christine and Giorgio and note down:

1 how Christine welcomes Giorgio.
2 how she asks for the reasons for Giorgio's application.
3 how she tells him that it is not necessary to take notes.
4 how she explains the reason for the length of the course.
5 how she promises to give him an answer soon.
6 how she says goodbye.

17.2   Finalizing the details

Before she circulates the final programme for the trainees, Christine Louis sends a letter to all the people who have been selected. In the letter, she asks each trainee to fill in a short questionnaire about their specific interests.

Work with a partner. Imagine you are going on the training programme. Fill in your answers and be ready to say why you made these choices.

---

page 3

and it would be very helpful if I could have your answers to the following questions. I will then process your answers and finalize the programme. This should be ready by the end of May.
We plan to have a number of outside speakers on the course. Please indicate which subjects would be of interest to you. Please put a cross (x) by any subjects which you would definitely not be interested in.

MANAGEMENT BY OBJECTIVES

INTERNATIONAL MARKETING

CREDIT CONTROL

FINANCE FOR THE NON-ACCOUNTANT

STAFF DEVELOPMENT AND TRAINING

NEGOTIATING CONTRACTS

SELECTING THE RIGHT STAFF : INTERVIEWING TECHNIQUES

CROSS-CULTURAL CONTACTS

Any other suggestions: ....

....

We will also be arranging visits to local industrial and commercial companies. Which of the following would you like to visit? Please choose up to three visits.

COMPUTER SOFTWARE COMPANY

SHIPYARD

ENGINEERING COMPANY PRODUCING MACHINERY FOR THE PAPER-MAKING INDUSTRY

RESEARCH AND DEVELOPMENT UNIT INVESTIGATING THE USES OF FIBRE OPTICS

FACTORY ASSEMBLING AND DISTRIBUTING TV SETS FROM PARTS IMPORTED FROM MALAYSIA

REGIONAL HEAD OFFICE OF NATIONAL BANK

SILICON CHIP PRODUCTION COMPANY

SCOTTISH DEVELOPMENT BOARD

Any other suggestions: ....

....

17.3 Cross-cultural communications

1 At the training course in Scotland, one of the outside speakers is Robert Quinn, a professor of International Studies at Glasgow University. Listen to the first part of his talk and say if these statements are **true** or **false**.

1 If you speak good English, you can do business deals anywhere in the world.
2 We need to understand the habits and expectations of a culture if we are understand the people.
3 Robert Quinn has never lived in the United States.
4 The American pace of life is fast.
5 Americans do not want to make lifelong friends of everyone they meet.
6 People in America feel equal to each other.
7 Americans are very interested in other cultures.
8 Crime is a big problem in the United States. Visitors have to be extremely careful.

2 Now listen again to the beginning of the talk. While you are listening to the tape, look at this tapescript. Some words have been added to Robert Quinn's talk. Cross out the extra words.

> Now, as you may all know, I am interested in cross-cultural communications
> and the different kinds of problems there are when people from different
> cultures meet one another. I'm sure in your time here in Scotland you have
> come across lots of examples of this. A lot of people think that all you have to
> do is learn English, Business English, and then, hey presto! you can go out
> there anywhere in the whole world and start doing deals. Well, I'm ...

3 How about your culture? First of all, answer these questions by yourself.

1 Do you normally shake hands when you meet a business partner for the first time?

2 At an important business meeting, how long is it before you start to talk about the business itself? What subjects can you talk about before getting down to business?

3 When do you give a partner your business card?

4 What hospitality do you normally offer a business partner?

5 How long is it before business partners call each other by first names – after one meeting, several meetings or never?

6 The invitation to the reception says eight pm. When do you arrive?

7 Do you pay a tip to
a) taxi drivers?   b) hotel staff?   c) railway staff?   d) waiters?
e) hairdressers?

If the answer is 'yes', how much do you pay?

● Now compare your answers with your partner's answers.

17.4   Success guaranteed

Here is a not very serious article about how to succeed in your office. Read it and do the tasks which follow.

So you want to be successful at work?
We're here to tell you how.

First, tidiness. Did you know that the higher you are in an organization, the tidier your office should be? When you start out, make sure you put up lots of urgent messages on the wall next to your desk. That way people will see how hard you're working. But as you progress, untidiness can be seen as a sign of inefficiency. Lee Wassermann, the head of MCA Records, used to visit all the offices late every evening and throw any loose paperwork into the bin. 'If you can't get it done before you leave,' he told his executives, 'you can't be doing it right.'

Never, ever throw away papers in your filing cabinet. They may take up a lot of space, but if you decide to throw them away, it's absolutely certain that you'll need them the very next day. The film producer, Sam Goldwyn, realized this. His secretary once asked him if she could destroy the files that were more than ten years old. 'Sure,' he said, 'but keep copies.'

If you wish to avoid making a decision, either send a memo or set up a committee to conduct an 'in-depth study'. If you actually want to reach a decision, toss a coin. Yes, seriously! When the coin is in the air, you will realize how you want the coin to land and the decision will be made.

If you want to get on in the office, first improve your job title. After all, 'administrative communications executive' sounds much better than 'post clerk'. If promotion is out of the question, try for a rise instead. Here, the basic rule is: never be afraid to ask.

In the 1950s, Tommy Docherty played alongside the great footballer, Tom Finney, for Preston North End, at that time one of the most successful English football clubs. Both received the maximum wage of £15 during the season, but in the summer Docherty used to get £2 less than the great man. Docherty complained to the manager that this was unfair. 'But you're not as good a player as Finney,' he was told. 'I am during the summer,' replied Docherty. He got his rise.

1   Complete these sentences, using information from the text.

1 An untidy desk is an advantage for a junior employee

because ....

2 An untidy desk is a disadvantage for a manager

because ....

3 You should never throw away papers in your filing cabinet

because ....

4 If you really want to make a decision, toss a coin,

because ....

5 You should try to improve your job title because ....

6 Tommy Docherty got a rise because ....

2   There are some useful phrasal verbs in the text. Find the phrasal verbs
which mean :

1 begin *(paragraph 2)*.
2 stick/fix papers on a wall *(paragraph 2)*.
3 use *(paragraph 3)*.
4 establish *(paragraph 4)*.
5 improve your position *(paragraph 5)*.

3   Discuss these questions in pairs or small groups.

1 Do you think a job title is important?
2 Do you think memos or committees should be used to avoid
making decisions?
3 How do **you** reach decisions?
4 How would **you** ask for a rise?

17.5 On the spot

Discuss with a partner what you would say in these difficult situations.

1 You are in a restaurant. You've just received the bill, but you are sure it's too high.
2 You pick up the telephone, but you can't hear the other person because the line is so bad.
3 It's 2.45 pm. You suddenly remember that you had an appointment at 2.30 pm on the other side of town. You telephone to explain.
4 A customer is telephoning to complain. He is very angry and is speaking so fast that you can't understand him.
5 You're invited to a cocktail party by an important client. But you can't attend because you've already accepted another invitation.
6 In your office, you come face to face with someone you think you have met before, but you can't remember her name.
7 You're having dinner in a restaurant abroad with a foreign colleague. The food is unfamiliar to you and you don't know what to choose.

8 You're on a business trip overseas. Your contact offers to spend an evening with you showing you around his city. You want to stay in your hotel and write up some important reports.
9 A departmental meeting is still going on after the time you expected it to finish. You have another important meeting to attend.
10 You have left your diary in a customer's office. You have a flight to catch in half an hour. You telephone to explain.

Language focus – Used to

1 *Lee Wassermann* **used to** *throw any loose paperwork into the bin.* This was his custom over a long period and it helped to improve his company's efficiency. But he's no longer head of MCA Records. He doesn't do it any more.

We use **used to** to show that we regularly did something in the past, but that we no longer have the same habit. Here are some examples:

1 *Professor Quinn* **used to** *live in the USA, but he's based in Glasgow these days.*
2 *We* **used to** *have departmental meetings on Wednesdays but we had to change to Fridays because management meetings are now held on Wednesdays.*
3 *We* **used to** *have a sales office in Manila, but it was closed in 1987.*
4 *This part of the factory* **used to** *be the Despatch Department. As you can see, it's now a production area.*

2 Look at this text. Decide whether to put the **Present Simple tense**, the **Past Simple tense** or **used to** in each of the gaps.

The company .... *(be called)* Abbot Engineering (UK) now but it ....

(be called) Caledonian Electronics before Abbot Electronics .... *(take)* it over.

We .... *(change)* a lot of things when we .... *(move)* in. For example,

they .... *(deal)* mainly with the UK market. There .... *(be)* no Export

Department at all at that time, so of course we .... *(have)* to set one up

immediately.

We also .... *(decide)* to change the layout of the site. The car park

.... *(be)* over there where the new administration block now .... *(be)*.

The road communications to Glasgow and down through England .... *(be)*

terrible, but when they .... *(built)* the motorway, everything ....

(improve) very quickly.

But, of course, you .... *(know)* about all that, don't you? You ....

(live) in Glasgow for a while, didn't you?

UNIT 18   *Overheard*

In this unit you will:

- discuss and deal with rumours.
- read and write memos.
- read about big city traffic problems.
- talk about how things work.

18.1   Late at night

1 You are visiting Digital Communications in Newbury, England from Excel Europe to discuss some technical improvements in DC's products. By chance, you overhear George Harman, a Product Manager, making a call on the telephone. You shouldn't listen, but you do!

1 What's he planning to do?

2 What do you think is the problem for DC?

3 What would **you** do if you overheard a conversation like this in your company?

2 George Harman is a key person in DC. He has a lot of technical information which could be useful to a competitor. When Philip Mason, George's boss, hears the rumours, he is determined to find out the truth.

Listen to George and Philip's conversation, and answer these questions.

1 How does Philip introduce the subject of George leaving DC?
2 How does George feel about his present job?
3 How definite are his future plans?
4 What does Philip ask George to promise not to do?

18.2 An exchange of memos

1 Philip Mason decides to inform Andrew Jarret, DC's Personnel Director about George Harman's plans. Here is Philip's memo.

MEMO
STRICTLY CONFIDENTIAL

To: Andrew Jarret
From: Philip Mason
Date: 24 March 19—
Re: George Harman, Product Manager

I understand from George Harman that he is planning to resign and take up employment with a rival company. As you know, he has been involved in some advanced development work which is essential for the success of our new communications systems.

   Not only is it important for him to continue his work for you and us but it could also be very damaging if he takes all his technical know-how and experience to another company working in a similar field.

   It seems that he has been offered a higher salary by our competitors. I think we need to set up a meeting very soon to discuss how best to handle this matter. As soon as we have agreed a policy line, we will need to interview Harman himself and resolve the situation as soon as possible.

Answer these questions about the memo.

1 Has Philip discovered which company approached George Harman?
2 Why does Philip want George to stay with DC?
3 What does Philip want to do about the situation?

2 Here is Andrew Jarret's reply. From what you already know, fill in the missing words.

MEMO
To: Philip Mason
From: Andrew Jarret
Date: 25 March 19—
Re: George Harman, Product Manager

Thank you for you memo dated yesterday.

It is true that Harman is involved in some very important ....

work. The success of our new communications ....

depends very much on his .... Some of the knowledge he

has would be very .... to a .... company. I feel he

should stay at least another six months or even one year if we can

arrange it. I will be in my office all day tomorrow. Can we meet to

.... the best way to handle this .... ?

Meanwhile, I enclose a copy of Harman's contract of employment

which shows clearly that he has to give twelve weeks' ....

18.3 George's future

1 Work in pairs. One of you is Andrew Jarret. The other is George Harman. You are going to meet to discuss George's future. You must try to reach an agreement. At the end of the discussion, George must decide whether to go or stay with DC.

Student B You are George Harman. Go to page 137 for your information.
Student A Here is your information as Andrew Jarret.

George has worked on the new communications system for four years. Two young technicians trained by George know nearly as much as he does about the system.

George could take his knowledge to a rival company working on a similar system.

You can offer George a maximum of $500 per month extra salary. He receives $1,950 per month at present.

You can offer one week's extra holiday.

Excel, your parent company, wants George to stay with your company to complete his project.

---

2 Now write a very short memo from Andrew to George with details of your meeting.

18.4 Big city traffic problems

1   Before you read the article, write down as many words as you can think of
connected with driving in a big city? What do you think these people
would say about the problem?

A private motorist
A lorry driver
A policeman
A politician
An ambulanceman

Now read the article and answer the questions which follow.

A PERMIT TO ENTER CENTRAL LONDON?

THE METROPOLITAN POLICE Commissioner, Sir Peter Imbert, suggested yesterday that private cars might be required to have permits to enter central London during peak hours.

Peter Joslin, Chairman of the Traffic Committee of the Association of Chief Police Officers and Peter Bottomley, the junior minister at the Department of Transport, said Sir Peter Imbert's suggestion should be taken seriously as a future option.

The Automobile Association (AA)* rejected the idea as impractical but supported Sir Peter's desire to find solutions to the daily crush of London's traffic.

Sir Peter said London's traffic was now so heavy that motorists would have to face some restrictions. He gave the example of Singapore where cars are allowed into the centre at peak hours only if they are carrying at least two passengers.

More than 2.5 million vehicles travel every day on London's 8,600 miles of road and motorway. At present, there are only 800 traffic policemen in the whole of London. At peak hours an estimated 190,000 vehicles are on the move and more than 2.5 million parking tickets are issued every year.

Both Mr Joslin and Mr Bottomley said other schemes could include in-car meters registering journeys through electronic checkpoints in roads.

The Royal Automobile Club (RAC)* believed money would be better spent on improving some major junctions and the North and South Circular roads, building bypasses for busy centres and providing better public transport.

*The AA and RAC are organizations which represent private motorists.

1 What are the reactions of the following to Sir Peter Imbert's suggestion?
a) The RAC
b) Mr Bottomley and Mr Joslin
c) The AA

2 What do **you** think the solution is?

2 Make five sentences which are true of the article using the table below.

1 Sir Peter Imbert	**felt**	in-car meters should be introduced.
2 Mr Joslin	**believed**	money would be better spent on providing better public transport.
3 Mr Bottomley	**said**	cars might have to have permits to enter London.
4 The AA	**suggested**	permits were impractical.
5 The RAC	**thought**	the new ideas should be taken seriously.

18.5 Pronunciation

Look at these words from the first part of this unit and underline the stressed syllable.

1 personnel
2 telephone
3 experience
4 damaging
5 employment
6 technical
7 agreement
8 discussion
9 definite
10 confidential
11 interview
12 yesterday

18.6 On the spot – asking for explanations

1 Listen to this conversation about the functions of a machine. Write down the phrases used to ask for an explanation of how it works.

2 Here is a list of some useful phrases. Match the questions and answers.

1 What's this for?
2 What does this do?
3 What does the green light mean?
4 Why is that thing bleeping?
5 What do you do if it won't work?

A Call the engineer!
B It turns on the machine.
C Because something is wrong.
D It means the machine is ready.
E Measuring the temperature inside.

3 You have just received a manual for a new machine. You are talking to the sales engineer. You don't understand:

1 the diagram on page 11.
2 the difference between the SD2 and SD3 models.
3 what *digitalized* means.

4 where points A1 and B1 are on the drawing.
5 where to switch it on.
6 what to do if it overheats.
7 how to remove the outer casing.

● Ask for explanations!

4 Today's office is full of gadgets. Work with a partner. Explain to someone new to your office how **one** of these things works or what it is for.

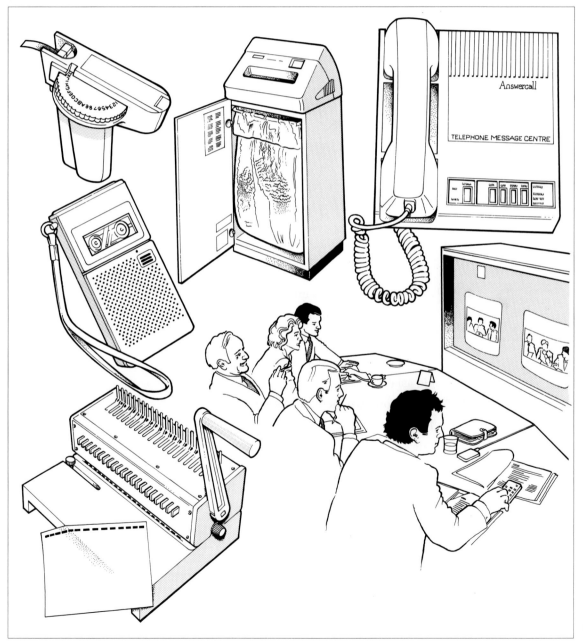

Language focus – Reporting

1 Verb patterns are very important when we are reporting people's ideas and opinions. Knowing the introductory verb, e.g. **tell, say, explain, suggest,** is not enough. We need to know how the sentence can continue. Here are some important verb patterns used in reporting.

1 He	says suggests believes feels agrees thinks	(that) we should do something immediately.	
2 He	suggests recommends	sell**ing** off Digital Communications.	
3 She	asked advised told instructed ordered wanted	me Mr Smith her secretary	to tell them.
4 He	explained to me showed me	how to do it.	

2 Change these sentences into reported speech.

1 'This is how you operate the computer terminal.'

She showed ....

2 'Please send the report as soon as possible.'

He asked ....

3 'Why don't we increase the price?'

He suggested ....

OR

He suggested ....

4 'In your position, I would do absolutely nothing.'

He advised ....

5 'Can you send a copy of the report to Personnel, please?'

He wants ....

6 'I think you should go for the South American market.'

She believes ....

7 'The best way to check the figures is to start at the end.'

He explained ....

This year ... Next year

In this unit you will:

- attend Excel's annual conference.
- find out how to summarize and generalize.
- meet conference delegates socially.
- talk and read about the future.

19.1   Arriving at the conference

1 This year the Excel Europe Annual Conference is being held at a luxury hotel overlooking Lake Lucerne in Switzerland. Christine Louis and Klaus Jensen are arriving at the conference. Listen to their conversation with the hotel receptionist.

Note down:

1 their room numbers.
2 the times for breakfast and dinner.
3 the special facilities at the hotel.
4 the arrangements for the Excel conference.
5 details of the hotel's business centre.

2 There are many different ways of asking questions politely. Listen again to Christine Louis and Klaus Jensen talking to the receptionist and complete the questions.

1 .... reservations?

2 .... filling in these forms?

3 .... see your passports as well?

4 .... where the Excel conference is being held?

5 I've parked my car at the front of the hotel, just outside.

.... all right there?

6 By the way, ... breakfast?

Over to you **3** You are also attending the conference. When you arrive at the hotel in Lucerne, you have to do these things:

- tell the receptionist your name and why you're in Lucerne.
- spell your name.
- ask about meals.
- ask about the telex and fax facilities.
- find out about the swimming pool and sauna.

How would you do all this? Work with a partner.

19.2 The President reports

1 David Latour, the President of Excel Europe, is reporting to delegates to the Annual Conference on Excel's performance over the past year. Listen and note down what he says about:

1 unsuccessful companies in the Excel Europe group
2 investment
3 the sales and distribution offices
4 the most successful single product

2 David Latour then goes on to talk about plans for the next two to three years. Note down Excel's plans and **how** the company will achieve them.

1 What is Excel planning to consolidate?
2 What does Excel want to expand?
3 What is Excel hoping to rationalize?
4 What is Excel hoping to develop?

3 Here's a list of nine personal aims. Work with a partner. Choose five of them (or add your own) and discuss how you could achieve these aims. Use **by** plus a verb with **-ing**.

1 become a millionaire
2 improve your physical fitness
3 achieve personal happiness
4 win the respect of friends and colleagues

5 start your own business
6 find the meaning of life
7 become famous
8 help other people
9 improve your social status

4 Match the verbs and the noun phrases in these two lists taken from David Latour's speech.

1 to finalize
2 to expand
3 to rationalize
4 to take on
5 to keep up with
6 to consolidate
7 to launch

A more marketing staff
B an advertising campaign
C details
D new technology
E Excel's activities
F production systems
G Excel's market position

19.3 The holiday that's out of this world

1 If you had the chance, would you take a trip on a spaceship? Read this article and find out about the holiday that really is completely different!

THE HOLIDAY THAT'S OUT OF THIS WORLD

A tour operator in London is offering the ultimate package holiday - a trip into space for £29,200 all in. Four Britons have already paid the deposit. Twickers World, specialists in faraway destinations, is offering 10-hour trips in a specially designed passenger spacecraft from Cape Canaveral in Florida every Thursday from 1994.

The package includes at least five earth orbits, custom made flight suits, 'fine dining' and a view of the world as a small sphere.

The spacecraft, designed to take off and land vertically, is being developed by Maxwell Hunter II, former chief planner of the Lockheed Rocket and Space Company.

Yesterday, Mrs Hedda Lyons, a director of Twickers World, said that the Challenger disaster had had little

impact on bookings. 'Surprisingly, we have had more interest since the disaster,' she said.

The Twickers World brochure, which reassures nervous clients of the spaceship's 'exacting safety standards' states: 'You board the vehicle as you would a jet aircraft. You can either choose to remain strapped in your seat during 'Zero G' or get up and float about to experience weightlessness. You have your own window to view the flight and record the trip with spectacular photographs.'

Seven minutes after take off and 1000 miles down range from the Cape Canaveral launch site, the spacecraft goes into orbit. For the next eight or so hours, passengers will circle the earth at least five times.

Re-entry takes an hour, with the

thrusters fired for landing at 17,000 feet. Final course corrections are made and the spacecraft glides down towards the landing site.

The 20-seater spacecraft is to be built by Pacific American Launch Systems of Seattle.

2   Find the information.

1   How much does the trip cost?
2   How long does each trip last?
3   When will the trip be available?
4   What does the package include?
5   Has the Challenger disaster made people more or less interested in space flight?
6   What can you choose to do during 'Zero G'?
7   What happens during re-entry?

3   Ask your partner.

● Do you think the price of the trip is fair?
● Would you go on the trip?
● Do you think this idea will be successful?
● Do you believe that the spacecraft is completely safe?

19.4   On the spot 1 – at the conference

You are a delegate at the Excel conference. You are going to make contact with other delegates at the conference. First, you will need an Excel identity.

1   Write your name (it could be your real name or you could make up a new name) on a label, so that everyone can see who you are.

2   Make up the following information about your new identity:

● job title
● place of work
● number of years with Excel
● reason for attending the conference
● personal details (family, nationality and so on)

3   Now imagine it is coffee time between sessions at the conference. Circulate among the delegates until you find someone you would like to talk to.

● Introduce yourself.
● Ask your partner where s/he comes from.
● Find out about his/her job.
● Ask what your partner thinks of the conference.
● Answer your partner's questions.
● Arrange to meet again later.

4   Now, still with your partner, find another pair of delegates. Introduce your partner and tell the other delegates something about him or her.

19.5   On the spot 2 – the end-of-conference party

1   Attending a conference means meeting people you haven't seen for a long
time. Often the first part of your conversation with an old friend or
colleague is about the time since you last met. Imagine you haven't seen
your partner for the last twelve months. Find out everything that has
happened to him or her during that time.

Here are some useful phrases:

How are you?
How is your wife/husband/family?
What have you been doing?
What are you doing now?
Do you remember ...? How is he/she?

2   Conferences are a time for talking about the past. But they're also about the
future. Work with a partner again. Find out what your partner would really
like to be doing in a year's time. Wish him/her good luck.

Here's how you wish someone good luck.

Good luck with all your plans.
I wish you the best of luck.
I hope all your plans work out.
Good luck in the future.

Language focus – The general and the specific

1 David Latour in his speech was not giving exact information about Excel's performance. So he used words and phrases which are **general** in meaning.

Here is a list of phrases:

In general, *For the most part,* *Generally,* *Mostly,* *Overall,* *On the whole,*	*profits were very good.*

Sometimes we want to show that there are exceptions. We can use **particularly** and **especially** to highlight a good example. We use **although** to introduce part of a sentence which gives information about an exception.

Study this paragraph.

In general, sales were very good, **especially** in Europe and the Middle East. **Overall**, profits were up, **although** there were some problems in the US market. **On the whole**, the results are very good, **particularly** for the radio data transmission systems.

2 Fill in the gaps in this paragraph.

...........................(1), our products have been more successful this year,

...........................(2) we have had some difficulties with delivery. Our high-

technology systems have been very popular,...........................(3) the X15

series. This series sells well all over the world, ...(4) in Latin

America. ....(5), we can be very pleased with our performance

this year, ...(6) it's always possible to improve!

"Keep up the good work, whatever it is, whoever you are."

20.1 The Suggestion Scheme

Jacques Belloc, Director of Human Resources at Excel Europe, recently attended an international conference on suggestion schemes and their value to companies. What do you know about suggestion schemes? Does your company run such a scheme? How is it organized?

Here is a handout prepared by Jacques Belloc from notes that he made at the conference. Read the handout and complete the task below.

1. *Medium-sized British foods manufacturer*
   Improved working relations. Helps employees to identify with aims of company... increased efficiency and productivity.
   Definitely saves money in estimated ratio of 4:1 (Savings: expenditure).

2. *Large German car manufacturer*
   Large scheme (5 full-time staff to run it. Total workforce 10,000)
   Scheme is cost-effective. Savings of over $2m last year.
   Top prize $25,000 and US holiday.
   Publicity essential + clear formula for awards, especially the big ones, (e.g. they work on the basis of employee getting 50% of first year savings, less development costs over three years).

3. *Small Italian plastics company*
   People often nervous about making contributions. Must be uncomplicated. Needs hard work by management to keep schemes going.

4. *Large Swedish electronics company*
   Publicity essential, especially at the start. Very important to have continued interest and pressure from all management/supervisors to keep up level of contributions.
   Difficult to evaluate all suggestions especially those connected with improvements in working conditions, but important to recognize all contributions, not necessarily in cash, e.g. every contribution rewarded with prize up to $10.00; employees choose their own prize from selection of small items: gadgets, cassettes, T-shirts, toys, etc.

5. *Medium-sized Finnish chemicals company*
   Workforce of 600. Total of 162 suggestions in Year 1. In Year 4, 2,500 received, i.e. over 4 per person. Total profit on scheme of approx $700.000. Success depends on keeping the scheme simple. Exercise book in rest room. Employees write down ideas/draw diagrams. Open for everyone to see and discuss. Gives workers a feeling of involvement in the company.
   Selection committee of both management and workers, to agree on awards.

Which companies mention the following? Write down the number of company - 1, 2, 3, 4 or 5.

1 a formula for calculating large awards	Company ....
2 publicity	Company ....
3 cost-effectiveness	Company ....
4 a selection committee	Company ....
5 working relations	Company ....
6 a simple system for recording suggestions	Company ....
7 the role of management	Company ....
8 prize money	Company ....

● Now list the benefits which are mentioned in Jacques' notes.

129

20.2 A meeting

 1 You are asked to attend an informal meeting called by Jacques to discuss the suggestion scheme in operation at Excel Europe. Jacques is going to report on the conference he attended. What points do you think he is going to make? Make a list of them.

Now listen to the report and tick off the points as you hear them. Are there any other points not on your list?

 2 The suggestion scheme has now been in operation for two years at Excel. Listen to Jacques talking about Excel's scheme and note down the following information.

1 Number of suggestions received in Year 1 ....

2 Number of suggestions received in Year 2 ....

3 Total number of people employed ....

4 Total savings made ....

5 Value of top prize ....

3 Jacques gives you a copy of Excel's policy document on suggestion schemes. Read this extract which describes the different stages of the scheme.

> There are suggestion boxes, clearly labelled, in every department, or section on the factory floor. Forms are kept beside the box. Employees fill in the form, with details of their proposal and an indication of the benefits they think it will give. The forms are collected each month by the head of each department or section who chooses those which s/he thinks are likely to show some benefit and passes them on to the Personnel Department. It is the responsibility of the Assistant Personnel Manager to consult other departments where appropriate, for example the relevant technical department, as well as the Financial Department. All suggestions requiring large investment must be passed to the Board of Directors for approval. All prizes are decided by the Personnel Department; awards are made on a quarterly basis and there is a first, second and third prize. Their values depend on the contribution to the company in terms of financial savings, efficiency and productivity.

Complete the flow chart to show the different departments and people involved in the scheme and their role.

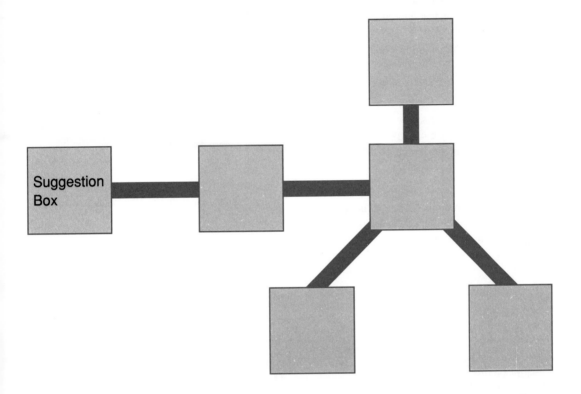

4 Work in pairs and discuss the Excel scheme. Make notes of any possible reason for the disappointing results; the handout from the conference may help you to identify some of the problems. How could the suggestion scheme be improved? Report back to your group on your findings with your reasons and your comments.

20.3 What a good idea!

On the next page is a number of suggestions received from your department in Excel. You are on the selection committee which decides which suggestions are worth an award. Discuss each of the suggestions. What will the benefits be if you decide to invest in them?

Now choose a short list of **three** only and prioritize them. Explain to the other selection committees the reasons for your final choice. Which single suggestion should get this month's first prize?

Suggestions received by selection committee

1 I would like to see a coffee machine installed on each floor for everyone on that floor to use. At the moment the coffee is made by one of the secretaries. Everyone goes into this office to get their coffee as it's so good. This disrupts her working and annoys everyone else in the office.

2 Could we please have some basic training on what to do if someone has a heart attack?

3 The main production block (Block A) is at least 100 metres from Block C (the main office block). We would like to see a covered walk-way built linking the two blocks.

4 We like pictures on the walls, but we do not like all the new abstract pictures in the Reception and the corridors and the canteen. Can we have some nice, interesting pictures e.g. people, landscapes..?

5 Why do senior managers receive the daily newspapers and specialist journals? Can I suggest that daily papers and magazines are made available to everyone and not circulated only to senior managers? There is space at the top of the stairs on the first floor for a seating area and a table where anyone could go and read them.

6 I have noticed that even in cold weather some people have their office windows open. It would save money if each office area had an individual thermostat to control the temperature. At the moment all offices are heated to the same temperature and this does not suit everyone.

7 As a secretary in the department I make all the travel arrangements for three colleagues through an outside travel agency. This takes up a lot of my time on the phone. I'm not sure if we are necessarily getting good value from them either. I would like to suggest that as our company is involved in a lot of overseas travel it would be a good idea to centralize all travel arrangements. We can set up our own internal office, or maybe a travel agency could have an office on site here.

8 All managers should do their own typing of reports, especially technical reports on their word processors.

9 Waste paper should be collected from offices for recycling. We tried this before but nobody took any notice and the idea was dropped - can we please try again?

10 I suggest that office staff are allowed to leave an hour earlier on Friday afternoons, and have a shorter lunch break (15 minutes less) on other days.

11 The company makes a lot of profit. Isn't it time that we gave some of this cash to charity on a regular basis and not just at Christmas when we have a party for old people in the area? The company could, for example, sponsor one charity throughout the year.

12 We would like to have one fifteen-minute break for every three hours worked. At the moment, in the offices we do not have official breaks except for lunch. This is especially important for those of us who spend a lot of time working with VDUs, as we get headaches and eyestrain if we work too long without a break. This time should be included in the paid hours of work.

Student B

Unit 1

1.2 On the way

Here is your information about Milan.

Milan
Attractions:
Cathedral, Castle Sforza, Galleria Vittorio Emanuele II (shopping arcade),
La Scala opera house, fashionable shopping streets
Distances: Florence 250km / Rome 450km / Turin 120km
Population: 1,000,000 (approx)
Economy: banking, fashion, engineering and chemical industries

Unit 2

2.5 On the spot

You are calling from the Holiday Inn in Amsterdam. Give Student A this information.

Confirm hotel booking for Miss Fernandez of Excel in Madrid: 1 single with shower for three nights (14-16 May inclusive) at Holiday Inn, Amsterdam
Tel: 631 2309 Tlx: 24071 HOLIAM NL, Cost: $95 per night.

Unit 3

Language focus

Fill in your diary for the week ahead. Some appointments are already fixed. Then with Student A find a time when you can both meet to discuss next year's budget.

MON ....

TUE *1100 Monthly routine meeting*

WED ....

THU ....

FRI 1530 *Swedish agent: meeting about plans for next year*

1930 *Dinner*

Unit 4

4.2 Two potential representatives

Find out about Far East Trading and give Student A information about Asean Enterprises.

	FAR EAST TRADING	ASEAN ENTERPRISES
contact		*Mr Khan*
experience of agency work		*8 years*
no. of employees		*50*
no. of regular customers		*850*
no. of sales staff		*15*
marketing expertise		*works as consultant*
contact with European companies		*limited*
impression		*dynamic*

Unit 7

7.1 A tour of the factory

Tell your partner about the production process.

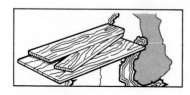

WOOD IMPORTED FROM FINLAND

THE KITCHEN FURNITURE SYSTEM

STAINLESS STEEL FITTINGS PRODUCED IN POLAND

UNITS MADE UP ACCORDING TO INDIVIDUAL CUSTOMER SPECIFICATION AND PACKAGED IN SWEDEN

ASSEMBLED ON SITE

7.5 **On the spot – taking a telephone message**

Give this order over the phone to Student A in the Sales Department.

Company *BRENOCON*   Contact name *GIORGIO*
Contact phone *EXTENSION 408*

Reason for call:

Quantity	Reference	Description
1000	*BG 77/6*	*Printed circuit boards*
500	*PA 53/9*	*Printed circuit boards*

Delivery

As soon as possible to: *BRENOCON factory in Koblenz, West Germany*

Invoicing/payment

As before, 30 days credit

Comments *Please send drawings of the boards at the same time*

Unit 8

8.1 **Reporting to the USA**

Describe the PD15.

PD15	SPECIFICATION
Size:	18cm x 11.25cm x 2.5cm
Power:	110-120 volts
Speed:	215 operations per second
Working life:	$3\frac{1}{2}$ years
Working temperatures:	5-45 degrees Centigrade
Price:	2,450 FF

8.2 **Phone calls in July and August**

Student B   Give Harold this information.
Figures for July
PD14 $20,525
PD15 $18,775
PD16 $6,950
JCAL $72,500
Problems: Late delivery of some SD shipments.
Fall in value of peseta against US dollar.

Student A   Give Harold this information.
Figures for August
PD14 $19,805
PD15 $18,625
PD16 $7,345
JCAL $66,750
Problems : No new orders because of holiday period.

Language focus

Are you dynamic?

Key

8 - 10 YES You really are dynamic. You're determined to be successful, even if it means hurting other people. You're only happy when you're active, at work or socially.

4 - 7 YES You are well balanced. Your career is important to you, but so is a stable home life and a steady routine. You'll be successful in the end but it will take time.

0 - 3 YES You are definitely undynamic. Your idea of a fun evening is sitting watching TV with a cup of tea. Wake up! There's a lot going on in the world. Don't let other people take charge. Stand up for yourself!

Unit 11

11.2 Discussing the details

You are Markus Bold.

> You want free technical training at Excel in Boston for your sales engineers.
>
> You want a 24-hour 'hot-line' emergency telephone number to call if your customers have any technical problems.
>
> You want to meet Excel technical staff regularly (every six months) to discuss new developments and products.

11.3 What's missing?

Ask your partner for the information to complete this contract.

The Principal, [................], will supply the Agent, Bolito Automotive, with up to [................] worth of goods during each trading period of twelve months. The Principal will pay [................] commission on all goods sold. Commission will be paid annually in January. The Agent will be the sole representative of the Principal in the states of California and New Mexico. All insurance will be paid by the [................], who will also bear 75% of the advertising and promotion costs.

Unit 12

12.2 **Suzie Taylor interviewed**

You are Suzie Taylor. Use your notes to answer Bill Timm's questions about the Indonesian project.

> Contract for Excel to supply Indonesian government with EP120X electronic communication system. Government minister responsible is Mr Benny Suharna, Minister of the Interior.
>
> Value of contract: initially $1/_2$ billion, but with training, after sales service etc could be $3/_4$ billion.
>
> System will be used by Indonesian Army to link active army units. Officers will have small hand-held transmitters.
>
> Power: solar + batteries
>
> Special security system (codename Silentman) means that no one outside can listen in to conversations.
>
> System tested by US Navy over five-year period. Already sold to three Middle East governments.

Unit 18

18.3 **George's future**

Here is your information as George Harman.

> An American company has offered you $750 per month extra salary, but the job is based in Holland and you'd prefer to stay in England if possible. Your current salary is nearly $2,000 per month.
>
> The American company wants to develop a system similar to the Excel communication system.
>
> Your job title at the moment is Product Manager. You would like to become Projects Director, if you stay with DC.
>
> You want two weeks extra holiday per year to spend with your wife and three children.
>
> You want the opportunity to take a month's unpaid leave, possibly every two years, to follow your favourite hobby, ocean sailing.